What readers are saying about "Catholic to Christian":

"Your story is a beautiful, wonderful thing that should go to show everyone just how powerful the Holy Spirit can be."

"Thank you for sharing your journey, I truly pray that it can be an enlightening story and blessing to others."

"I find that your story is inspiring, and I hope that you and your family continue to grow in faith and wisdom in reaching out to people."

"The truth has been revealed to me in the scriptures and through prayer. I have to pass it on to those loved ones that are being misled. I ask that you keep me in your prayers, and thank you again for sharing your story."

"I experienced a huge feeling of relief after reading your story and thank you for taking the trouble to share your experiences."

GearPress
PO Box 321
Riverview, Florida 33568-0321
www.gearpress.com

Original Cover Photo by: BigStockPhoto.com
Cover Design: S.C. Slawin/GearPress

ISBN-13: 978-0615949772
ISBN-10: 0615949770

LICENSE NOTES

Published by GearPress. For more GearPress publications, visit us on the Web at:

http://www.gearpress.com

S. C. SLAWIN

CATHOLIC TO CHRISTIAN

**An Exploration of Catholicism and
One Man's Journey from Darkness
into God's Wonderful Light**

A GEARPRESS PUBLICATION

To My Dear Readers:

I'm an independent author, which means that I choose to write and publish my writing without the benefit of agents or contracts or any sort of guarantee of compensation. Times are not easy for independent authors, but those of us who enjoy writing for ourselves and for readers like you value that independence.

I wanted to take a moment to ask you for your help. One of the most important things an independent author can have are <u>reviews</u>. Reviews help readers decide whether or not they should make an investment in reading a book like this one. All reviews are very important to authors, the most glowing praise and the most scathing comments are equally welcomed.

I know that what I've written here isn't for everyone, and I truly respect all opinions on my work. If you believe in and support independent authors like myself, then I ask you to *please* take the time to rate my book where you acquired it.

Most sellers such as Amazon make filing your review of this publication very easy. It usually takes less than one minute of your time. Whether you enjoyed this book from start to finish or whether you couldn't stand to read another word, won't you please take just a few moments and write a brief review? Your assistance in this matter is vital to the on-going success of independent authors.

Thank you,
S.C. Slawin

For My Brother Chris

Even though you're no longer with me here, it is because of you that this book is possible. Thank you, brother, for leading me to Christ.

Table of Contents

CHAPTER ONE
Introduction

All praise, honor, and glory to God, my Father in Heaven.

If you are a practicing Catholic or someone who is interested in Catholicism, then I sincerely hope that you find my personal story inspiring and helpful. Even if you're not Catholic but are interested in learning more about eternal salvation, I truly hope that you will take the time to read my message completely. At times as you read the story documenting my personal journey of faith, you may feel uncomfortable or be tempted to stop reading, probably because some of what I have to say here is foreign to you or possibly contrary to what you've been taught in the past.

Believe me, I completely understand that feeling and those concerns. At one time in my life if I had read a story like this one, I would have felt precisely the same way. Instead of abandoning the story of my discovery of true faith, I ask you to trust that the Lord has led you to read this for a very good reason.

I have written my story out of pure love for my Father in Heaven, and out of love for His children here on earth. I was guided by the Holy Spirit in developing this message and it is written to help spread the truth of God's Word. There is nothing here designed to deceive or mislead anyone in any way, because what I share with you here is my true story, the story of my receiving the gift of eternal life through the grace of God.

Most of all, I tell you this: if you doubt anything that I write here in regard to Holy Scripture and the Gospel, then please, *do not* take my word for anything. I am but a mere human being who is, without a doubt, flawed. God and His Word, however, are perfect. Rather than take my word that anything I say here regarding the Gospel is truth—in fact, rather than take anyone's word—I encourage you to sit down and read the Holy Scriptures for yourself, for His Word contains the complete truth about His plan for everlasting life.

I do not expect anyone who reads this to swallow my words whole; I wouldn't and I don't expect that of you.

However, what I will ask is that even if my story makes you feel uncomfortable, even if you disagree with every single point I raise, please continue to read my account all the way through until the end. I would appreciate it if you would read what I have written with an open mind. Then take what I've written and put it to the test.

> *"Prove all things; hold fast that which*
> *is good."*
>
> - *1 Thessalonians 5:21*

* * * * *

I was born in 1961 to very faithful Catholic parents who never missed mass. As an infant I was baptized in water to wash away my original sin and to initiate me into the Church. For those who are unfamiliar with Catholicism, the baptizing of infants is a normal practice. I was raised in the Catholic Church and through my parents and my catechism, I was taught everything I was told that I needed to know about Catholicism. I made my first confession and communion as a youngster, like most other normal Catholic children. Later, as a teenager, I was confirmed (*confirmation* is a sacrament in Catholicism) and through that sacrament I ascended into being a full-fledged adult in the Catholic Church.

By my estimation, I was a prime example of a *cradle Catholic.*

But for me, just being a faithful part of the congregation wasn't enough. At a young age I found that I wanted to do more than simply sit in a pew at mass and pray with those around me. Because of my desire to be a more active participant in my church, I volunteered to be an altar boy and was trained to serve on the altar. Altar servers participate in the mass by assisting the priest during the service. I spent many years faithfully serving, and in time I was elevated to the lead position, overseeing all of the altar servers in my parish. I trained new servers, coordinated the schedule and other activities of the altar boys, interfaced with other people of leadership in our parish, and eventually took an active role in other committees, groups, and functions of the church, including adult education.

In time, I also became a Sunday school (CCD) teacher, preparing the young children of our parish to become an active part of the Catholic Church, and I specifically helped them learn what was necessary for them to take part in their first communions. Once I reached my twenties I took on yet another role in our parish, becoming a lector, so that each weekend I stood on the altar and read the Scripture readings to those in the congregation. In time, I was recruited by the head of the church RCIA program (*Rite of Christian Initiation for Adults*) to become an instructor. As an RCIA teacher, I was educating converts from other faiths as well as those who were not already involved in any established organized religion who desired to become a part of the Catholic Church.

After forty-four years as a devout Catholic, my entire life until that point, I had no doubt in my mind or in my heart that the Catholic Church was the one true church. I believed this sincerely because I was taught that the Catholic Church was the church that Christ Himself had established on earth. The Catholic Church taught me that the apostle Peter was the rock on which Christ founded the Catholic Church, and Peter was recognized by the Catholic Church as the first Pope (more on this later).

I was certain, without any doubt, that the teachings of the Catholic Church were the correct teachings for all Christians, and that everything I was told by the Church was absolute truth. I knew then that whatever the Catholic Church told me about the Holy Scripture was exactly what God wanted me to know. For me to think otherwise at that time for even a moment would have been simply ridiculous.

I went to church faithfully, I was baptized in water as an infant, I followed the Catholic doctrine and traditions, and I regularly went to confession and communion. I was taught that the communion wafer I received at mass, a small round piece of unleavened bread, was truly the body of Christ

Himself. Catholics are taught that the communion wafer is transformed from simple bread into Christ's *actual* flesh at each mass through the doctrine of transubstantiation. The Catholic doctrine says that during the mass, bread and wine are transformed into Christ's real flesh and real blood, even though the outward appearance of them remain unchanged.

I knew, because I was taught by my Catholic educators, that if I faithfully followed the rules of the Catholic Church and continued to receive forgiveness for my sins, through absolution dispensed by a priest during confession, I would have a chance to enter into God's Heavenly Kingdom when I died. I was absolutely convinced that as a faithful, practicing Catholic, I was truly as Christian as anyone could be. In fact, since Catholics are taught that the Catholic Church was established on earth by Christ Himself, many Catholics believe that the Roman Catholic Church is, in fact, the one and only true Christian church.

I learned, because the Catholic Church told me so, that if I lived my life as a faithful Catholic then through my taking part in confession and communion, and through the penance that I paid for my sins, along with my good works, I could receive a place in Heaven.

CHAPTER TWO
Faith Under Fire

One day I was watching television, and while changing channels I happened to stop on a local program featuring a preacher. I didn't know anything about this man, or what his religious affiliations might have been. This preacher was very passionate about the Holy Scripture, and I was briefly captivated by his enthusiasm. At one point this unnamed preacher stated that he had a special warning for all the Catholics who were viewing his program. This preacher stated that many teachings of the Catholic Church are, in fact, contrary to the Bible itself. He declared that Catholics who followed the doctrines of the Catholic Church were being misled. He stated that most likely those who followed Catholic teachings had not actually been saved.

I knew that this TV preacher couldn't be right. After all, I was born into the Catholic Church, the church that Christ Himself had established. I was baptized as an infant, I took an active role in the mass and in my church, and I followed the teachings of Catholicism. Certainly what this particular preacher had to say did not at all reconcile with my beliefs or what I was taught, but I wasn't naive, I was well aware that attacks on the Catholic Church weren't anything new. The beliefs and practices of Roman Catholicism had come under fire for centuries. It wasn't only this random TV preacher dispensing ominous words of warning against the Catholic Church, there were plenty of other forces out there taking aim at Catholicism. Throughout my life the leaders of the Catholic Church and my parish had warned me that "Catholic bashing" had been on the increase. These warnings had gotten even more urgent and intense at that time in my life, since the Catholic Church was enduring an onslaught of well-deserved criticism. This criticism was primarily focused on the horrible misdeeds and abuses of children at the hands of Catholic priests and others in leadership positions within the Church.

For some reason that I had yet to understand, I found that this particular preacher's message was something that I needed to investigate further on my own. I certainly didn't have all of the answers myself, but as a good Catholic I decided to do what the Church had told me to do when my faith was in question: I decided to turn to those within my church who were thoroughly educated in the teachings of Catholicism. The very next day I took the time to speak privately with the pastor of my parish about the negative things I had heard this unnamed preacher say about Catholics and Catholicism.

After mass was over and the altar was cleared and prepared for the next service, I went to the sacristy. The sacristy is the room where the priest and altar servers dress and where the items used during the mass are kept. As soon as the priest was ready, the two of us took a stroll together around the grounds of our parish, which was situated on the site of a local Catholic school. As we walked, we passed a statue of Mary, and I questioned my priest about the message I had heard on television just a day before.

"Father," I asked. "Why did this TV preacher say that the teachings of the Catholic Church sometimes differ from the Holy Scripture?"

The priest listened intently to my question. He could clearly see that I was troubled by the television broadcast. Still, despite my very serious concerns, he was fairly terse with his reply. While my pastor didn't spend any time making any specific references to Scriptures or to teachings of the Catholic Church, he told me that I should ignore what the TV preacher had said. He explained to me that this was yet another example of "Catholic bashing". The priest told me that it was very obvious to him that the TV preacher didn't actually understand the Catholic Church at all, and that any Bible passages the preacher may have quoted must have been taken out of context. Even if the Holy Scripture did *appear* to differ from the doctrines of the Catholic Church, my pastor said that those differences were easily explained. This is because the leadership of the Catholic Church had been given the power to interpret and even modify the Holy Scriptures, which allowed the leaders of the Roman Catholic Church to create and change doctrine and rules for its followers.

My priest told me in no uncertain terms that I should trust only in the leadership of the Catholic Church for everything I needed to know about salvation. He dismissed the television preacher, telling me that the Holy Scriptures can be very, very confusing and are often misinterpreted by the layman. He said that only the leaders of the Catholic Church have the divine inspiration necessary to sort out all of that confusion and to truly understand the Word of God. He assured me that I need not worry about this television preacher and his message. He was, my pastor explained, misguided and misled by evil forces and his attempts to sway Catholics away from the teachings of the Church was evidence of his evil intent. I should stand firm, my priest told me, and reject everything I might be told about the Holy Scriptures from sources other than the leaders of the Catholic Church.

My priest made it clear that I was a confirmed Catholic and an RCIA teacher and I should trust in what the Catholic Church had taught me. He assured me that while it was natural to question my faith at times, by placing my trust solely in the leaders of the Catholic Church, I could confidently and safely believe in the teachings of the Church. Besides, he told me, as a leader in my parish I needed to set the example for others. Part of that example was to display complete and total faith in the Catholic Chuch.

My pastor wasn't at all interested in what the TV preacher had to say about the Holy Scriptures or his opinions about the Catholic Church and its traditions and teachings. My priest, a sincere man to be sure, had tried to reassure me about my faith without delving too deeply. Somehow the priest's answer left me with even more questions. Still, despite my lingering doubt, at that time I continued to trust in the Catholic Church, my church, and I continued to rely on it and its leaders for guidance in how I should practice my faith. I was successful in holding at bay that small sliver of doubt that the television preacher had raised in me.

My brother Christopher, a name that means "Christ Bearer", was six years younger than me. He was raised exactly as I was by our faithful, devout Catholic parents. He made his first confession and communion, he served on the altar as I did, he was confirmed in the same way I was, but unlike me he never aspired to any particular leadership role in the parish. He was a faithful Catholic for many years, but over time it appeared that something was changing in him. As an adult he eventually stopped attending mass regularly, only showing up on special occasions such as certain holy days.

Chris was steadily falling away from the Catholic Church and my parents and I were deeply concerned for him. At first we felt that he simply wasn't interested in matters of faith, but later we learned that there was much more to it than that. In time, to our dismay, his lack of participation in the Catholic Church got so bad that my poor brother had to be nearly dragged to our church one particular Christmas Eve for midnight mass. That was the last time that he and I attended a service at our parish together, apart from my father's funeral.

As time went on, Chris started making attempts to try and sway me from my Catholic beliefs. Obviously, as a very devout Catholic, I resisted his efforts. Still, I wondered why he was openly attempting to get me to leave the Catholic Church. He tried again and again to lead me away from what I had been taught all of my life, but I stood firm and argued with him about matters of faith over and over again. Chris questioned me frequently about salvation. He questioned me about the Holy Scriptures. He questioned where I had decided to place my trust, and he asked whether I trusted in the leadership of the Catholic Church or if I trusted in Christ.

The answer to my brother's question was obvious to me: I felt that as a devout Catholic I obviously trusted in Christ, but I also trusted in the Catholic Church and the men who made up its leadership. It seemed so obvious and straightforward to me. Why could I not trust in both God and man, equally, for my Salvation?

I had always dismissed most of my brother's arguments, especially when he told me that it was wrong to put any of my trust in the human leadership of the Catholic Church for salvation. He tried to explain to me that it simply wasn't possible to trust in the leaders of the church *and* to trust fully in Christ. He used many passages from the Holy Scriptures to try and illustrate to me where my claim of being able to trust Christ and the leaders of the Catholic Church equally was a flawed belief. I found his arguments, all backed by Scripture, to be fairly credible, but at the same time I found them very hard to swallow. Let's face it: my opinion at that time in my life was that my brother Chris was a man who didn't even go to church with us any longer, yet he was trying to tell me—an altar server, head altar boy, a CCD teacher, a lector, an usher, and a certified teacher in the Catholic Church's RCIA program—this so-called truth about the Catholic Church and the Holy Scripture. He was attempting to lecture me, a religious teacher, about salvation? About where I should place my trust in order to receive the gift of eternal life? The mere notion was utterly ridiculous to me.

Besides, where did this non-practicing Catholic learn so much about the Scriptures?

After many, many more discussions with my brother Chris, discussions that had lasted literally for years, I learned that he had been following Bible discussions led by a man named Dr. Hank Lindstrom, the pastor of the local Calvary Community Church. Dr. Lindstrom was also the host of radio and television programs for Bibeline Ministries. It took some more time, but eventually my brother convinced me to at least listen to some of Dr. Lindstrom's messages.

Dr. Lindstrom certainly seemed to be a very devoted and intelligent man who hosted radio and television programs. He made it his mission to share the Gospel. After listening to his programs, I knew for certain that Dr. Lindstrom was sincere, and as a devout Catholic I felt that at worst this gentleman was simply misguided or misled. There was no doubt that Dr. Lindstrom had spent many, many years immersing himself in the Holy Scriptures, that much was clear because of his amazing depth of knowledge and his ability to quote any passage from the Bible. While Dr. Lindstrom's views on the Word of God may have differed in some ways from what the Catholic Church had taught me, in a few other ways they were quite similar.

To be clear, Dr. Lindstrom was not the same preacher I had seen on television before. To this day I still don't recall the name of the television preacher I had asked my parish priest about. Hank Lindstrom was not the TV preacher who originally had preached to me against the teachings of the Catholic Church.

"But who is this Dr. Lindstrom, anyway?" I wondered. "He seems well-meaning, but maybe this guy is wrong about some of the things he's telling my brother and others about the Holy Scripture. When it comes to the issues of faith, how could my brother know for certain that Dr. Lindstrom was right? How could anyone know that the person telling them about the Word of God is not leading them astray?"

One thing that I knew for certain is that the truth—the proof—can only be found in one place: in the Holy Scripture.

> *"All scripture is given by inspiration of*
> *God, and is profitable for doctrine, for*
> *reproof, for correction, for instruction*
> *in righteousness".*
> **- 2 Timothy 3:16**

And to be quite frank, despite my reservations, Dr. Lindstrom seemed to agree that it was right for me to have my doubts. In fact, every time I heard him speak he told everyone who listened not to simply take his word for anything he'd said about the Holy Scripture. Dr. Lindstrom stated plainly that we who heard his messages should pick up our Bibles and read it for ourselves.

Unlike some other organized religions, the Catholic Church didn't place a great deal of emphasis on bringing a Bible to church with us. This is because during each mass the Church decides which parts of the Scriptures will be read to the congregation, and those readings are provided in a booklet called a *missalette*. In fact, we were told that we should not even follow along with the readings in the missalettes. Instead we were advised to lay aside our booklets and simply listen as the readings were read for us.

I know that my brother Chris truly loved me and cared about me and wanted me to have eternal salvation. At first I had taken his efforts to convince me to consider an alternative to Catholicism as simply well-meaning but misguided advice. Over time, however, as my brother became more insistent that I should put aside some of what I was taught by the Catholic Church, I started to become concerned that he was actively attacking and attempting to destroy my faith.

Deep inside I still had to know that my brother was sincerely trying to help me, but at times I could only see his attempts to sway me as attempts to tear me away from the

Catholic Church. I saw his arguments as attacks on what I believed to be the one true church, the church that I had been taught was founded by Christ Himself. It was, too be quite frank, very disturbing and troubling to me.

CHAPTER THREE
The Opening of My Eyes

In what seemed like a last-ditch effort to finally open my eyes, my brother bought me a book called *Understanding Roman Catholicism* by Rick Jones. When he gave the book to me, I dismissed it without so much as opening the cover. I absolutely did not want to read it at all. I was actually concerned about being given yet another piece of anti-Catholic propaganda that was aimed at attacking my church.

According to the description, the Rick Jones book claimed to explore the differences between Roman Catholicism and true Bible-based Christianity. The book said that it showed ways in which the teachings of the Catholic Church differed from the Holy Scripture. I felt that this book, which reportedly exposed the differences between Catholic teachings and Scripture, could in fact be a very dangerous publication. It was a book that I actually *feared*.

Because of my fear, rather than read the book for myself I gave it to the head of our parish's RCIA program. This was another person in our parish I had looked to for leadership and guidance in matters of faith. I didn't want to be somehow inadvertently misled by this book, so I asked her to take it, to read it on my behalf, to analyze it in depth, and to please let me know why this particular book was in error about the Catholic Church. She took the book, kept it for some time, then later returned it to me.

Our RCIA leader's analysis of *Understanding Roman Catholicism* was short and simple: it wasn't to be taken seriously. At all. Clearly, she said, the writer doesn't understand Catholicism *or* the Bible. As before when I asked my pastor about the television preacher, the answer I had received from someone I trusted for spiritual guidance and leadership had left me with even more lingering questions.

That evening we had a scheduled meeting of the RCIA instructors. I told the others about my brother Chris and his attempts to lead me away from Catholicism. The other teachers were dismayed. All of us prayed together that my brother would reject these "false teachings" and return to the Catholic Church.

Not long after that night I was told by our diocese that I, along with the other teachers at all levels in our parish, would be required to take a solemn oath regarding our roles as Catholic educators. This was called the *Oath of Fidelity* and I was convinced that it would be an important step in my service to the Church. I believed at that time that taking the oath was the right thing to do.

All of the parish teachers were required to sign a written oath card and to publicly affirm that we would only teach precisely what the Catholic Church had decided we could teach. We were required to recite this oath before the rest of the parish during mass. It was required that we swear to use only the educational resources provided by the Church, and we pledged that we would not use any other teaching materials. Among the list of approved materials I found one very important teaching tool for Scripture conspicuously missing: the Holy Bible.

I can fully appreciate that the Catholic Church wants to ensure that only approved teaching and approved instructional materials are used by their teachers. Certainly any organization would want to ensure a level of consistency and control over what is being taught in their classrooms. But as I understood it, the Bible itself was not on the list of approved materials I was allowed to use as part of my RCIA instruction. Up until that point we had used the Bible in our

RCIA classes, and we consulted it often. However, because the Bible was not on the list of approved materials, our RCIA leader removed the Bible that we kept in our classroom.

The Holy Scriptures in the form of a Bible was apparently something that my *Oath of Fidelity* to the Church prevented me from using as a teaching tool. While I understood the Church's desire for control, excluding the Bible was still somewhat unsettling to me. I certainly wasn't a Bible expert by any means, but one thing I did know for certain is what the Holy Scripture did say about instruction:

> *"All scripture is given by inspiration of God, and is profitable for doctrine, for reproof, for correction, for instruction in righteousness".*
> - *2 Timothy 3:16*

It was the exclusion of the Holy Bible that really started making me think much harder about the leadership of the Catholic Church. As a teacher, I faced a decision about the *Oath of Fidelity*. We were told that if we chose not to take the oath we could no longer remain in our roles as Catholic teachers. I felt strongly that I wanted to help spread the Word of God, and I convinced myself that I would probably regret losing the opportunity to continue teaching. I felt that over time I could eventually reconcile my concerns about the Bible being excluded as an approved teaching tool, so I decided that I would sign the oath. Along with the other Catholic educators in our parish I took part in the public proclamation of that same oath before the whole congregation. Despite my affirmation, in my heart I knew that without the Bible as an integral part of my teaching, I actually didn't fully agree with the terms of that oath.

Affirming the *Oath of Fidelity* without agreeing to it due to my reservations sparked a real pain of conflict inside me. That pain caused me to begin to explore the Holy Scriptures outside of the guidelines of the Catholic Church. Specifically, I began to investigate whether there was truly a difference between being Catholic and being Christian. I prayed and prayed and prayed on this issue while I continued to work through my personal research.

As I explored the Scriptures for myself, my brother Chris continued to point out to me things that concerned him about the teachings and practices of the Catholic Church. He spoke to me at length about instances in which Catholic practices and the Holy Scriptures appeared to be in disagreement. About that time it was the beginning of the new year, early one January, and he asked me if during the month of December my parish had displayed Christmas trees in the church. Naturally we had, in the church and on the altar itself, as it was the church's custom. In fact, our parish (like most other Catholic parishes) had quite a number of Christmas trees, all of them decked out in shiny gold and silver ornaments and cute decorations that the children in the catechism classes had made. I told my brother Chris this, and he in turn asked me to pick up my Bible and research one passage in particular:

> *"Thus saith the LORD, Learn not the*
> *way of the heathen, and be not*
> *dismayed at the signs of heaven; for*
> *the heathen are dismayed at them. For*
> *the customs of the people are vain: for*
> *one cutteth a tree out of the forest, the*
> *work of the hands of the workman,*
> *with the axe. They deck it with silver*
> *and with gold; they fasten it with nails*
> *and with hammers, that it move not."*
> *- Jeremiah 10:2-4*

So upon reading Jeremiah 10, I was left to wonder about the message. It appeared, at least on the surface, that Jeremiah was warning us who followed Christ that we should not behave like the "heathen" and cut down a tree, affix it to the floor, and adorn it with silver and gold decorations. To me, that description certainly sounded like the traditional Christmas tree as we know it, and Jeremiah was clearly warning us not to behave as the pagans did. There, in the Scriptures, it was written that we shouldn't erect trees in our homes and adorn them with decorations.

In regard to Jeremiah 10, some historians might tell you that pagans of that time would cut down a tree, carve it into a statue, fasten it to some place in their home, and then adorn the statue with items made of precious metals. I've found that there is plenty of debate among certain historians as to whether or not the modern Christmas tree is considered a pagan symbol. What cannot be denied is that it was, indeed, the custom of the people and the Catholic Church to have Christmas trees on display in the church and up on the altar itself. Because of the disagreement over the symbolism of the modern Christmas tree, because of this current *gray area* of opinion, I managed to convince myself that the pagan statues of the time were *not* the same thing as a traditional Christmas tree and that Jeremiah was not warning us against decorating and displaying such trees.

I was convinced that I was doing nothing wrong by putting up and decorating a tree in my home. I was convinced that *my* Christmas tree was not against the words of the Holy Scripture. I told my brother Chris that when I put up a Christmas tree in my house that December, I was not engaging in pagan tree worship at all. No, I was simply decorating my house as was the customary tradition of the season. My tree and its decorations meant absolutely nothing as far as Jeremiah 10 was concerned. It was no more than custom and tradition; my Christmas tree carried no non-Christian meaning whatsoever.

Confident that I had thoroughly defended my position, my brother asked me a question that I found very difficult to answer:

> *"If Jeremiah were to visit your house,*
> *or even Jesus Himself, what do you*
> *think they would have to say about*
> *your tree?"*

That was a very interesting question. I had to pause and carefully consider what my brother Chris was *really* asking. When I did, I realized that I was allowing myself to rationalize my actions into a "gray area" of Holy Scripture. By attempting to dismiss the Scripture, I was creating my own loophole. I was trying to apply my own interpretation of what the Holy Scripture meant, instead of simply distancing myself from something that could be considered a pagan symbol. Why would I do that? As a true Christian, wouldn't I want to eliminate pagan symbolism from my home entirely, regardless of the amount of debate over whether that symbolism is still relevant today?

In doing my historical research, I learned that long before the advent of Christianity, plants and trees that remained green all year long had a special meaning for people in the winter. Just as many folks today decorate their homes during the Christmas season with evergreen trees, ancient people hung evergreen boughs over their doors and windows. In fact, those people believed that these evergreens would keep away witches, ghosts, evil spirits, and illness. Therefore, my purely historical research seemed to support the argument that our modern Christmas tree was a modern-day version of a pre-Christian pagan tradition that was created to ward off evil.

It occurred to me that I should have taken the Holy Scripture exactly as it was written and said to myself: "Well, certainly there is no reason, other than custom and tradition, to put up this silly decorated tree in my house. So then why am I trying to talk myself into making it acceptable?"

Instead of simply receiving the Holy Scripture and behaving as it told me I should, I tried to convince myself that there was nothing wrong with my pagan symbol. I actually thought to myself, and I even said to my brother: "This tree means nothing to me." Sure, some people might see my tree and know that it had a pagan origin, but how many people could that really be? So what if I was skirting the edges of

Scripture by erecting a pagan symbol in my home every year? After all, this tree did not represent paganism or tree worship to me.

My brother then pointed me to another bit of Scripture, a passage that slammed shut the window on my comfortable little gray area where I was able to camp out for a while and rationalize my actions:

"Abstain from all appearance of evil."
- 1 Thessalonians 5:22

The Holy Scripture tells us here that we should not only avoid evil, but we should also avoid any *appearance* of evil. We should not even allow ourselves to put forth any outward appearances that would in any way be interpreted as being against the Word of God. Even if this silly tree meant nothing to me personally, I had conveniently forgotten that this pagan symbol was displayed in such a way that made it appear that I was supportive of pagan traditions, customs, and beliefs. Even though I wasn't a pagan, I was still displaying a symbol that is common to paganism. I was putting forth an appearance of evil, despite the Holy Scripture telling me that I shouldn't.

"But come on," I thought. "A Christmas tree is nothing more than a sign of the season! It's nothing more than an old tradition that has been around for hundreds of years. How harmful could such a simple old tradition actually be?" I told myself that tradition doesn't nullify the Word of God, it is simply a tradition that people had taken part in for years and years, nothing more. But then, at my brother's prompting, I discovered in the Holy Bible the Words of Jesus Christ Himself when he spoke to the pharisees:

> *"Thus have ye made the*
> *commandment of God of none effect*
> *by your tradition."*
> *- Matthew 15:6*

Now that is a very, very powerful piece of Scripture, and it gave me great pause. Christ Himself was clearly saying that a tradition (like my traditional Christmas tree) could render God's own Word *of none effect*. What? How is such a thing even possible? I suddenly became enlightened to the knowledge that it is entirely possible precisely because of my exact attitude toward Jeremiah 10. I was completely disregarding the Holy Scripture for my own reasons, for my customs and traditions, and therefore the Scripture was rendered of none effect *on me*.

I had not nullified the Holy Scripture itself, I had nullified the impact of the Scripture on me because I chose to disregard it. To put it another way, I'll provide a modern-day example: there may be laws against speeding in your town. However, those laws have no effect on people who speed. The law itself doesn't physically *prevent* speeding, the law (like the Holy Scripture) only has the appropriate effect on those who obey it. Drivers who disregard the law don't nullify the law, they simply nullify the law for themselves. In the end they nullify the effect of the law, but if they're caught they will pay the price for their disregard. Unlike human law, however, God always knows whether or not we keep His Word or disregard it for our own benefit.

Like the speeder in my example nullifies the effect of the law, I was, by my very own actions, nullifying the effect of the Holy Scripture. Not for everyone of course, but for myself.

Further, according to Mark's account, Jesus says to the pharisees:

> *"Making the word of God of none*
> *effect through your tradition."*
> *- Mark 7:13*

But not only was being immersed in this old custom and tradition harmful to myself, rendering God's Word of *none effect* for me, but it was also very harmful to my family. As the leader of our household, as the person who is responsible for ensuring that my family was true to the Word of God, allowing this tradition to persist in our house despite the admonition of Jeremiah 10, I was rendering God's Word of *none effect* for not only myself but for the rest of my family. Like the pharisees through their customs and traditions were rendering God's Word of none effect to their people, I was doing the exact same thing to my family. On top of that, I was blatantly displaying a pagan symbol in my home for anyone who visited our house to see, even if most people didn't realize those pagan origins.

It was then that I realized just how badly wrong I actually was. I realized, to my dismay, that I was allowing tradition and customs that were celebrated by my so-called "church" to render God's Word of *none effect*. I allowed the traditions of my church to allow me to rationalize my actions into gray areas of Scripture. In fact I should have realized that no such gray areas exist. The Word of God itself is clear, but these loopholes were nothing more than an invention of my own, or an invention of my church. This realization, my great epiphany, troubled me very much.

This, finally, was the opening of my eyes.

CHAPTER FOUR
A New Understanding

Once I had come to the realization that the customs and traditions of men could actually render the Word of God of *none effect*, I started to take my brother's words much more seriously. Sensing that the time was right, Chris then asked me about my salvation. He asked if I knew what I had to do to in this life in order to make certain that after my physical death I would assure myself of eternal life. I told him that there was actually no *assurance* that I knew of, but I was doing exactly what the Catholic Church had told me to do. I believed in God, I believed in Jesus Christ, I went to mass, I tried to live a good life. I did my best to observe His commandments, I confessed my sins in the confessional, I received my penance and then absolution from the priest, and I took communion. Outside of church, I tried to do good works. I tried to live right and avoid sin. As my church had taught me, even though I had no unending assurance of salvation that I knew of, I was doing all that I could to make a place for myself in Heaven. I tried my best to help others and to behave in what I believed was a "Christian" way.

Since I spoke of my belief in God and Jesus Christ, my brother Chris took that opportunity to talk to me at length about the word "belief". In the transliteration of the original Greek text, the word that was translated into "belief" in modern English actually came from the Greek word *pisteuo*. Pisteuo can be translated more accurately into English to mean "trust". Therefore, my brother explained, it is beyond simple belief but rather *trust* that is important to our salvation. He applied a very apt analogy to the chair at his desk at work. Chris pointed at the chair and said to me: "I believe in that chair. It exists, of course, and I believe it is real. However, more than simply believing in the chair, I also *trust* that it will hold my weight when I sit on it."

The distinction, a very important one, became clear to me through my brother's explanation of the original Greek augmented by his analogy. It was then that I knew that when reading the Holy Scriptures I can apply the word *trust* when I read the English word "believe" or "belief".

My brother Chris wanted to talk more with me about the practice of receiving communion at mass. Specifically, he asked me more about transubstantiation. Transubstantiation is Catholic belief that the sacramental wine poured on the altar and the communion wafer, a piece of unleavened bread, is really and actually transformed into the Body and Blood of Jesus Christ, even though their outward appearance remains unchanged:

> *"(1413) By the consecration the transubstantiation of the bread and wine into the Body and Blood of Christ is brought about. Under the consecrated species of bread and wine Christ himself, living and glorious, is present in a true, real, and substantial manner: his Body and his Blood, with his soul and his divinity (cf. Council of Trent: DS 1640; 1651)."*
>
> **- Catechism of the Catholic Church**[1]

This belief in transubstantiation is not considered by the Church to be an optional one for Catholics:

> *"Canons of the Most Holy Sacrament*

of the Eucharist: Canon 1. If anyone

denies that in the sacrament of the

most Holy Eucharist are contained

truly, really and substantially the body

and blood together with the soul and

divinity of our Lord Jesus Christ, and

consequently the whole Christ,[42]

but says that He is in it only as in a

sign, or figure or force, let him be

anathema."

- The Council of Trent Session XIII[2]

The Council of Trent says that anyone who denies the transubstantiation, anyone who says that the bread and wine are not actually and really transformed into the Body and Blood of Jesus Christ is *anathema*. By "let him be anathema" the Council of Trent is not literally pronouncing those who deny their canon as accursed or bound for eternal damnation as some protestants may believe. Yes, that is the etymological meaning of the word, but in this context the Council of Trent is using the word "anathema" to mean *excommunication*. Excommunication means removing someone from the body of the Church, literally it means banishment. Therefore, Catholic canon says that if anyone does not fully accept that the communion wafer—the Eucharist—is not truly, really and substantially the Body of Christ then they are to be excommunicated: they are not allowed to be a part of the Catholic Church. Because of the strength of the canon and language, this is a required belief.

Defenders of this particular canon refer to a very literal interpretation of Matthew as the basis of this belief:

> *"And as they were eating, Jesus took*
> *bread, and blessed it, and brake it,*
> *and gave it to the disciples, and said,*
> *Take, eat; this is my body. And he took*
> *the cup, and gave thanks, and gave it*
> *to them, saying, Drink ye all of it; For*
> *this is my blood of the new testament,*
> *which is shed for many for the*
> *remission of sins. But I say unto you, I*
> *will not drink henceforth of this fruit*
> *of the vine, until that day when I*
> *drink it new with you in my Father's*
> *kingdom."*
> *- Matthew 26:26-29*

My brother Chris sat with me and we discussed this particular part of the Holy Scriptures at great length. After a long discussion and prayer, I was enlightened to the fact that in this case I had to believe that Jesus was not being literal, that the cup of wine He held in His hands did not transform into His actual blood, and the bread He held in His hands did not transform into his actual flesh. How could I come to the conclusion that Jesus wasn't being literal? Because of Matthew 26:29 which I have included above, but defenders of transubstantiation often leave out of their argument. Immediately after Jesus speaks of the wine as a symbol of His Body, He Himself refers to that very same wine as "fruit of the vine". If it has literally transformed into His blood at that moment, He would have taken great care to refer to the contents of the cup as *His blood* rather than wine.

If you are a practicing Catholic, do you believe that the priest, through the Church's miracle of transubstantiation, actually transforms the communion wafer into the real Body of Christ before you receive it? If you can't believe that, according to the canon of the Catholic Church as affirmed by the Council of Trent, you cannot be a genuine Catholic.

And let me also tell you that even if you are a practicing Catholic and you believe this transformation is only symbolic, then you are actually among the majority of people who consider themselves practicing Catholics. According to a poll conducted by the Gallup organization, seventy percent of practicing Catholics surveyed did not believe that the Eucharist is actually transformed into the Body of Christ[3].

Does this mean that seventy percent of so-called practicing Catholics aren't actually Catholic at all? Technically, according to the Council of Trent, it does. However, I do not see the Catholic Church in any rush to excommunicate and banish seventy percent of its supporters.

This fundamental problem of belief does, however, point out a major misunderstanding among the majority of the followers of the Catholic Church. By their belief that the doctrine of transubstantiation is symbolic rather than real, these Catholics are denying the very most fundamental canon of the Eucharist, and therefore are engaging in a heretical belief according to leaders of the Catholic Church.

Holy Scriptures assures us that Jesus was, indeed, speaking figuratively about His Body and Blood. Here He refers to Himself as "the living bread":

> *"I am the living bread which came down from heaven: if any man eat of this bread, he shall live for ever: and the bread that I will give is my flesh, which I will give for the life of the world."*
>
> *- John 6:51*

Clearly Jesus indicates that the "eating of this bread" is

not the literal consumption of His flesh, but rather the consumption of His Word. His sacrifice of flesh is not that He gave His Body to be eaten, but rather that He gave His Body up to death on the cross to provide us eternal life. This consumption of His flesh must be symbolic, because He states that He will give His flesh for the life of the world, and common sense tells us that Jesus was not advocating that the world should convert to cannibalism in order to receive salvation.

If you consider yourself a practicing Catholic and you don't believe that the communion wafer dispensed at mass is actually transformed into the real presence of Christ's Body, can you continue to remain a practicing Catholic? More importantly, if you cannot accept this fundamental canon of the Eucharist, *should* you remain a practicing Catholic?

In Acts we read that Gentile followers of Christ were warned against the drinking of blood. Therefore, simple logic and Holy Scripture tells us that the belief in transubstantiation doesn't make sense:

> *"But that we write unto them, that*
> *they abstain from pollutions of idols,*
> *and from fornication, and from things*
> *strangled, and from blood"*
> *- Acts 15:20*

Jesus would never instruct his faithful to take part in such a forbidden practice.

Once I came to be enlightened that the doctrine of transubstantiation did not make sense when considered in light of Holy Scripture, the discussions with my brother Chris turned to confession and penance. My brother informed me that through my works I was trying to actively *participate* in my own salvation. True, but what is wrong with actively participating in my own salvation? Why is active participation in my own salvation something that I *shouldn't* be doing? Chris explained to me that through my self-participation I was, essentially at least in some part, trying to save myself. He shared more very relevant Scripture with me:

> *"For by grace are ye saved through*
> *faith; and that not of yourselves: it is*
> *the gift of God: Not of works, lest any*
> *man should boast."*
> *- Ephesians 2:8-9*

Here we are told that we are only saved by God's Grace through our faith. Very clearly the Word says that salvation cannot come from ourselves or our works:

> *"And if by grace, then is it no more of*

works: otherwise grace is no more

grace. But if it be of works, then is it

no more grace: otherwise work is no

more work."

- Romans 11:6

So why was I actively trying to help "save myself" through my works? And why would my church tell me that works, specifically confession, absolution and penance, were a necessary part of my salvation when the Holy Scripture clearly says that they are not?

What I was taught no longer made sense to me. I realized that the Holy Scripture says quite clearly it isn't works that will give me eternal life, it is only by God's Grace that I could be saved. Scripture says it as plain as it can be said: salvation is my free gift from God.

And then it really hit me: how could *anything* that I do in my life have more saving power than Jesus Christ's sacrifice on the cross? How could any works that I perform, or any works of the Catholic Church, or any actions at all that I might take, have any saving power that would eclipse the death of the Savior of the world? How can my actions wipe away any of my sin? How could anything that I do, as a mere human being, augment Christ's death for my sins?

You probably now see the answers to these questions

for yourself: our works cannot save us, our works cannot pay for our sin. There is only one conclusion that remained and that is the truth that we can, indeed, be saved only because it is God's will:

> *"By the which will we are sanctified*
> *through the offering of the body of*
> *Jesus Christ once for all. And every*
> *priest standeth daily ministering and*
> *offering oftentimes the same sacrifices,*
> *which can never take away sins: But*
> *this man, after he had offered one*
> *sacrifice for sins for ever, sat down on*
> *the right hand of God; From*
> *henceforth expecting till his enemies*
> *be made his footstool. For by one*
> *offering he hath perfected for ever*
> *them that are sanctified."*
>
> **- Hebrews 10:10-14**

The Holy Scripture was completely and abundantly clear, as stated unequivocally in Hebrews: it is by God's will that I am sanctified. No priest can take away sin. Christ's sacrifice was *for all sins forever,* and through God's Grace and Christ's sacrifice I am *perfected forever,* because I am sanctified.

For those who don't know, to "sanctify" means to "set apart, to be declared holy". When we understand the meaning of being sanctified, we understand God's Will as it pertains to our salvation. The Holy Scripture is telling us that faith in God will set us apart from others who lack that faith (we will be sanctified) and that the sanctified, those of us who have faith in God, are *perfected forever.* Forever is for all eternity, *perfected forever* means eternal salvation.

What a simple, wonderful plan God has for our salvation! In Acts, the Philippian jailer asked Paul and Silas what is required for salvation:

> *"Sirs, what must I do to be saved? And*
> *they said, Believe on the Lord Jesus*
> *Christ, and thou shalt be saved, and*
> *thy house."*
> *- Acts 16:30-31*

Here again we encounter the word "believe" and can substitute the more distinct word *trust.* Paul and Silas tell the jailer that he simply has to trust in Christ, nothing more. They said nothing to the jailer about any works that he had to do, any particular actions that he had to take, in order to receive eternal life. In fact, they immediately shared the Word of God with the jailer and his family and he and his entire house were saved.

> *"For by grace are ye saved through faith; and that not of yourselves: it is the gift of God: Not of works, lest any man should boast."*
>
> *- Ephesians 2:8-9*

If salvation were earned by my actions, then I might have reason to brag about what I had done to save myself, which is precisely contrary to the Holy Scripture. Think of a world where each of us was responsible for saving ourselves. Can you imagine the amount of public boasting and bragging that would go on from some of those who felt they had done the most to ensure their salvation?

To believe that we must actively participate in some way in our own salvation, to believe that we must do more than trust in Christ's sacrifice for our eternal life, is to believe that it is the sacrifice of God's only Son PLUS something more that is necessary to enter the Kingdom of Heaven. Yet the Holy Scriptures do not describe something more that is necessary for eternal life. Clearly we now know this is not God's will.

> *"He that believeth on the Son hath*

everlasting life: and he that believeth
not the Son shall not see life; but the
wrath of God abideth on him."
- *John 3:36*

Salvation is a gift. We can never, ever earn a gift, it is something that is given to us without regard to our own deeds. No one can earn a gift. If we attempt to earn a gift, then it would no longer be a gift but instead it would be a payment that we received in exchange for our work. If salvation was through works, our works would turn God's gift into a wage that was paid only to those who deserved it because of their actions.

We're humans. As humans, we're naturally skeptical. We have a difficult time in believing that we can receive something for nothing. Perhaps due to this skepticism as humans we need even further clarification of this very important distinction between God's Gift of eternal life and payment for our deeds. In order to find that clarification, we turn back to the Holy Scriptures once again, where the difference between salvation through faith and payment received for our works is made crystal clear:

"For the wages of sin is death; but the
gift of God is eternal life through Jesus

Christ our Lord."

- Romans 6:23

This is a very, very important distinction that those of us who were raised in the Catholic Church must come to fully understand in order to assure ourselves of eternal life. The Scripture makes it as plain as it possibly can. We can earn *wages* for sin, but everlasting life is a *gift*, something that we simply cannot earn. The punishment for sin is something that we can receive if it is *deserved*, while salvation is freely given to us whether we deserve it or not. In fact, the Holy Scripture says in no uncertain terms that none of us actually deserve God's Gift of everlasting life:

"For all have sinned, and come short of the glory of God"

- Romans 3:23

I was finally putting together all of the pieces of God's simple plan for my salvation. The Word of God tells us that there are two ends—life and death—and how each of those ends are achieved. Death (which in the Holy Scripture refers to spending eternity apart from God) is a wage (payment) that we can earn through our works, while life (eternal salvation) is a gift that is freely given, regardless of whether we deserve it or not. In fact, Holy Scripture makes is clear that all of us have sinned and none of us deserve everlasting life.

Works are not a part of the consideration when it comes to the gift of eternal salvation. Holy Scripture is again abundantly clear:

> *"But to him that worketh not, but*
> *believeth on him that justifieth the*
> *ungodly, his faith is counted for*
> *righteousness."*
> *- Romans 4:5*

To restate Romans 4:5 in plain language, the person who does no works but simply trusts in God (who justifies the wicked), that person's faith is counted for righteousness. Holy Scripture says quite clearly that works are not required to receive the gift of eternal life. And let's be quite frank: our own simple logic should confirm that truth for us as well. Gifts are not earned, they are given freely.

Once I understood the importance of this revelation I then began to seriously question the teachings of the Catholic Church. This concept wasn't the same as what I had always been taught. I was constantly told that in order to achieve a state of grace, I must go to confession and confess my sins, receive absolution from the priest, receive my penance and complete it, and then receive communion. Through my brother's help, through my own prayers and my own research into the Holy Scriptures, I learned that what I had previously believed was not God's plan. I finally knew that eternal death is something we can work for, while eternal life is something we can only receive as a gift through faith.

Only then did I fully understand the incredibly simple plan that God has for my salvation. My own actions could not save me and no offerings from any priest (see Hebrews 10, above) could take away my sin.

Of course others, like my fellow Catholic teachers, tried to convince me that I could only receive salvation through the Catholic Church, and through my actions in taking part in confession, absolution, penance and communion. Many tried to tell me that I had to participate in my own salvation. In fact, those who disagreed with my new understanding of Holy Scripture often quoted James, who famously wrote "faith without works is dead". Unfortunately, most people who quote James in this context are missing his point entirely: James never said that faith without works ceases to exist, he's simply saying that unless someone who has faith demonstrates their faith through their actions, their faith alone cannot inspire others to follow Christ. It's the same as hiding your light under a basket: the light itself doesn't go out—it still burns brightly—but no one outside of the basket can see it or benefit from it.

James writes:

> *"If a brother or sister be naked, and*
> *destitute of daily food, And one of you*
> *say unto them, Depart in peace, be ye*
> *warmed and filled; notwithstanding*
> *ye give them not those things which*
> *are needful to the body; what doth it*
> *profit? Even so faith, if it hath not*
> *works, is dead, being alone."*
> *- James 2:15-17*

James makes his intent clear when he refers to faith without works. If we do not demonstrate our faith by how we act toward others, then our faith is dead, which James further clarifies to mean "being alone". Note that James says that dead faith is faith that is *alone*, not faith that does not exist. Dead faith is still faith, but it is off to the side, by itself, not inspiring to others. Being alone means that the faithful who do not demonstrate their faith cannot inspire others.

These are powerful, powerful words.

The issue of eternal salvation being simply a free gift from God can be hard to accept, especially for those of us who were raised to believe that we have to actively participate in our own salvation. Those of us who were told that we had to make a place for ourselves in Heaven find it very difficult to accept that such a valuable thing as everlasting life can simply be given to us with absolutely nothing in return. But we must remember that the way of God and the way of humans are different. As humans we tend to think that things of such rare value require effort to attain, or that we must make ourselves in some way deserving. Instead, it is God's Will that we should receive eternal life as His free gift. The price of this gift is paid once and for all by the sacrifice of His Son on the cross.

But what if, despite all of this, we still somehow believe that works must be required for salvation? We simply need to turn once more to the Holy Scriptures where our Lord has erected the equivalent of a flashing neon sign explaining this concept that we humans find so difficult to accept.

In reading about the death of Christ on the cross, we can see, illustrated without any confusion, that it is faith and not works that will save us. We know that at the time of Christ's death He was crucified along with two malefactors, men who had been judged as lawbreakers and sentenced to die. Both of these malefactors had something to say to Christ as they were crucified beside Him:

> *"And one of the malefactors which*
> *were hanged railed on him, saying, If*

thou be Christ, save thyself and us.

But the other answering rebuked him,

saying, Dost not thou fear God, seeing

thou art in the same condemnation?

And we indeed justly; for we receive

the due reward of our deeds: but this

man hath done nothing amiss. And he

said unto Jesus, Lord, remember me

when thou comest into thy kingdom.

And Jesus said unto him, Verily I say

unto thee, To day shalt thou be with

me in paradise."

- Luke 23:39-43

Here we are told of two men, both sinners, who were crucified for their misdeeds. One mocked Christ and called for Him to save them all from death. The other recognized Christ's divinity and in that brief moment before his death, that man trusted that Christ was going to come into His Kingdom of Heaven. That trust in Christ is what saved the man, as Jesus said to him: "Verily I say unto thee, today shalt thou be with me in paradise." Hanging on the cross, that criminal had no opportunity to do any good works, to do anything to earn his way into Heaven, no time to do anything to atone for his sins. Indeed, he was judged a criminal and freely admitted that he deserved the punishment he was receiving. Yet his faith and trust in Christ is what allowed him to be with Jesus in paradise.

> *"After this, Jesus knowing that all*
> *things were now accomplished, that*
> *the scripture might be fulfilled, saith, I*
> *thirst. Now there was set a vessel full*
> *of vinegar: and they filled a spunge*
> *with vinegar, and put it upon hyssop,*
> *and put it to his mouth. When Jesus*
> *therefore had received the vinegar, he*
> *said, It is finished: and he bowed his*
> *head, and gave up the ghost."*
> **- John 19:28-30**

As John tells us, at His death, Jesus said: "It is finished". My brother asked me again to turn to the original Greek to get a more complete understanding. Through my research I found that the original word attributed to Christ at His death was the Greek word *tetelestai*. Tetelestai has been <u>literally</u> translated into the familiar phrase "it is finished". However, more importantly, I learned that the word *tetelestai* was also written on business documents or receipts in New Testament times to indicate that a bill had been paid in full. This connection between receipts and Christ's sacrifice would have been completely clear to John's Greek-speaking readers; it would be unmistakable to them that Jesus Christ had died in order to make *payment in full* for their sins.

If Christ paid for my sins, all of my sins, what more could I possibly do to add to that? What more could be expected? In what way could I contribute to my salvation that would have more saving power than God's only Son paying my sin debt in full through His death?

I talked to other teachers in the RCIA program about my epiphany and about the Holy Scriptures. I began to express my questions about what we were taught and what we were teaching. I was concerned about the fundamental differences between the Holy Scriptures and the teachings, the traditions, and most importantly the visible actions of the Catholic Church. I sought guidance from the other educators and our RCIA program leader. I told them about my brother's efforts to get me to put aside the Catholic Church's teachings and to rely solely on the Holy Scriptures for guidance in my faith. I told them about his advice that I should compare the teachings of the Catholic Church to the Holy Scriptures.

At first, the other RCIA instructors shook their heads in disbelief over what they were hearing. Then they expressed pity for my brother Chris because he had "fallen away from the Church". Next, they tried to comfort me and tell me that he was actually misguided and that Chris was simply being misled by someone who clearly didn't understand Christianity. They assured me that he had simply fallen in with the "wrong sort of people" who really couldn't possibly understand Holy Scripture. After all, they said, the Catholic Church reserved the authority on earth to interpret God's Word. They reminded me that I was taught that I had to place my trust in the Catholic Church. Surprisingly to me, their words meant nothing, because I was finally enlightened to the truth.

They prayed that my brother would have his eyes "re-opened" and he would come back to Catholicism. I bowed my head, but I did not pray with them, because I finally had received the full truth of God's plan for salvation.

There I was, despite my new realizations about the Holy Scripture, sitting with a group of people who were praying for my brother's return to the very organized religion that had to that point kept me from receiving the true Gift of Eternal Salvation.

I now had a new understanding. It was an understanding that at one time I had tried to deny, but I simply could deny it no longer. The power of God's Word was too strong. I knew then that I was finished with my former church.

For the first time in my entire life as a Catholic I began to seriously doubt that I was actually saved.

CHAPTER FIVE
The Powerful Message of Truth

My brother Chris then introduced me to the most powerful message I had ever heard about salvation. He gave me a CD called *How Permanent is Your Salvation?* and he asked me to listen to it. Actually, "asked" may be too mild a word, as I'm pretty sure he almost begged me to listen to it. I laid it aside and didn't think too much about it for quite a while, until one day I was heading for my car to drive to work. I wasn't sure at the time exactly why, but on that day I decided to pick up the CD and bring it with me. As I pulled out of my driveway, I put the CD into my car's player and began to listen.

The speaker was Dr. Hank Lindstrom, and the strength and conviction in his voice engaged me. It was a recording of a live event at which he was speaking about the permanency of eternal salvation, which Catholics know is contrary to what the Catholic Church teaches. The Catholic Church takes the position that salvation can be lost to mortal sin. As Catholics, we would need to turn to the church for salvation again through confession, absolution, penance and communion, or we will miss out on Heaven. Needless to say, Lindstrom's message wasn't at all what I was accustomed to hearing.

I soon found myself at the end of my twenty minute drive to the office, but I craved more information from Dr. Lindstrom and his incredible CD. I took it out of the car's player and brought it inside the office with me and listened to the rest of it as I worked. When the CD was finished, I wanted so badly to hear it again that I re-played it later that afternoon. When I left for the day I brought it back with me to the car again, and listened to this amazing message as I drove home to my family.

Dr. Lindstrom's simple message about the permanency of eternal salvation, each claim backed by clear references to the Holy Scripture, changed my life forever. Some of these references to Holy Scripture that prove salvation is permanent:

"Verily, verily, I say unto you, He that
heareth my word, and believeth on

him that sent me, hath everlasting life,

and shall not come into

condemnation; but is passed from

death unto life."

- John 5:24

The words in John 5:24 are the words of Jesus Christ Himself. Certainly none of us can presume to believe that Jesus Christ is a liar or would speak incorrectly on such an important topic as salvation. In fact, Jesus makes it as clear as can be. He states not only that those who come to the Father through Him *have everlasting life*, but in addition those who receive everlasting life *shall not come into condemnation*, but we are by God's Saving Grace *passed from death unto life*.

Moreover:

"All that the Father giveth me shall

come to me; and him that cometh to

me I will in no wise cast out. For I

came down from heaven, not to do

mine own will, but the will of him

that sent me. And this is the Father's

will which hath sent me, that of all

which he hath given me I should lose

nothing, but should raise it up again

at the last day. And this is the will of
him that sent me, that every one
which seeth the Son, and believeth on
him, may have everlasting life: and I
will raise him up at the last day."
- John 6:37-40

Again, the words of Jesus Christ make it clear that once we receive God's Gift of eternal life, we have it forever. Jesus says that *him that cometh to me I will in no wise* (in no way) *cast out.* Christ assures us that it is the Father's Will that of all of those who come to Him he will *lose nothing* (no one) and that He will *raise them up on the last day.*

"My sheep hear my voice, and I know
them, and they follow me: And I give
unto them eternal life; and they shall
never perish, neither shall any man
pluck them out of my hand. My
Father, which gave them me, is greater
than all; and no man is able to pluck
them out of my Father's hand. I and
my Father are one."
- John 10:27-30

And again, Jesus Christ tells us the truth about the permanency of our salvation. He says that to His sheep (His followers) He gives them *eternal life* and they *shall never perish.*

What an amazing assurance to have!

Those who don't believe in the permanency of salvation despite the evidence in Holy Scripture, evidence provided in the words of Jesus Christ Himself, will often argue that such an assurance creates some sort of loophole. Such an assurance, they contend, means that the true believer who trusts in Christ could go on to lead a sinful life and still have eternal salvation. But that's not a loophole. In fact, that's God's plan! God knows that we are sinful, He created us. He knows our imperfections and our failings, and He knows that as human beings we are prone to sin. That is why He sent His only Son to die on the cross to pay for our sins: past, present, *and future.*

I will say that I don't believe that the assurance of eternal salvation is a license to live a sinful life. In fact, I feel that those who truly trust in Christ are reborn. As Jesus tells us, through our rebirth we are transformed into people who have a desire to live as sin-free a life as we possibly can. That is, in part, because we are indwelt with the Holy Spirit.

Now regarding the *How Permanent is Your Salvation?* CD, let me be completely clear: Dr. Lindstrom didn't convince me that his information about the Holy Scriptures was unquestionably correct. In fact, he stated in his message that no one should take his word for anything he'd said. I put everything he said to the test. I went directly to the Bible and researched the Word for myself, and that's what I urge you to do as well. Dr. Lindstrom's message inspired me to seek the truth of God's Word, and I hope that my story will inspire you to do the same.

That was the incredible power of the message, and of Dr. Lindstrom's CD: he showed me exactly how simple God's plan for eternal salvation truly is. It wasn't Dr. Lindstrom's words that created the lasting impact for me, it was the Word of God that I researched for myself. Dr. Lindstrom simply presented the Word in a way that it hadn't been presented to me in the past, and he encouraged me to find out for myself rather than believe anything that any person told me.

* * * * *

The Catholic Church, the church of Rome, has attempted to reserve for itself the sole right to interpret Holy Scripture. The Catholic Church has decided that only it may decide the actual meaning of the Scriptures. While this stance is certainly beneficial to the Church of Rome (since it can decide what its followers are to believe), it isn't beneficial to people who are seeking the truth of God's Word. The Holy Scripture simply does not need to be interpreted for us, for if we place our trust in Christ alone and tell Him that we will no longer rely on the words of men to tell us the meaning of Scripture, we will have the counsel of the Holy Spirit. Then as we read God's Word we will have Him to help us understand its real truth.

Once I fully understood the simplicity of God's plan for salvation and how the Catholic Church has manipulated the Word of God to suit itself, I found myself rejecting the Catholic Church completely. I won't lie, that scared me at first. I prayed and prayed and prayed over my fears, and I asked the Lord Himself to guide me down the right path. I asked Him to lead me in the right direction, to help me make certain that I was now correct in my faith.

The Catholic Church, in an effort to continue to control and manipulate the Holy Scripture, contends that tradition is just as important as the Holy Scripture. Of course the Catholic Church would insist on that. Why? Placing so much importance on tradition ensures that the followers of the Catholic Church believe whatever the church says or does. But please don't take my word for it. You can confirm the Catholic Church's stance that their traditions are equal to Holy Scriptures by reading the *Catechism of the Catholic Church* from which I quote:

> *"As a result the Church, to whom the*
> *transmission and interpretation of*
> *Revelation is entrusted, does not*
> *derive her certainty about all revealed*
> *truths from the holy Scriptures alone.*
> *Both Scripture and Tradition must be*
> *accepted and honored with equal*
> *sentiments of devotion and reverence."*
> **- Catechism of the Catholic Church**[1]

So the Catholic Church insists that tradition and Holy Scripture must be accepted and honored as equal when it comes to Spiritual truth. It also says that the church can decide which traditions are worthy of being retained and which traditions can be abandoned. The church of Rome gives itself far too much power to completely shape the faith of its followers in spite of the Holy Scriptures. The Roman church empowers itself to decide for millions of their faithful what those followers should believe, even if their traditions happen to run counter to the Holy Scripture. However, as I have quoted previously:

> *"All scripture is given by inspiration of*
> *God, and is profitable for doctrine, for*
> *reproof, for correction, for instruction*

in righteousness"

- 2 Timothy 3:16

There may be many debates about the importance of tradition. But despite all of the debate over whether or not tradition should be integral to spiritual truth, we can turn directly to the words of Jesus Christ Himself to settle the issue about which is more important, Scripture or tradition:

> *"Then came to Jesus scribes and*
> *Pharisees, which were of Jerusalem,*
> *saying, Why do thy disciples*
> *transgress the tradition of the elders?*
> *for they wash not their hands when*
> *they eat bread. But he answered and*
> *said unto them, Why do ye also*
> *transgress the commandment of God*
> *by your tradition? For God*
> *commanded, saying, Honour thy*
> *father and mother: and, He that*
> *curseth father or mother, let him die*
> *the death. But ye say, Whosoever shall*
> *say to his father or his mother, It is a*
> *gift, by whatsoever thou mightest be*
> *profited by me; And honour not his*

father or his mother, he shall be free.

Thus have ye made the

commandment of God of none effect

by your tradition."

- Matthew 15:1-6

As I have previously discussed in this book, Christ tells us that the commandment of God can be made of *none effect* by tradition. Clearly tradition itself cannot nullify the Word of God, but it *can* nullify the Word of God for those who accept the rules of tradition rather than the Holy Scripture. Again, we have another very, very powerful piece of Scripture that speaks against the doctrine and practices of the Catholic Church.

Regardless of whether you believe tradition is important in your religion or not, no matter which side of the tradition debate you might be on, whatever you might say about this portion of Holy Scripture, at least one enduring truth must be accepted: by the Words of Jesus Christ, the traditions of the religious leaders were clearly subject to the Word of God, not equal to it as the Catholic Church insists it must be.

How can both Jesus and the Catholic Church be right? If you were asked to choose, who would you decide to trust?

The Catholic Church is wrong about tradition having equality with the Word of God. In light of this revelation, it was then time for me to make an important choice. My choice was that I could either believe in the teachings of the Catholic Church, the traditions and practices it promoted, or I could instead trust in Christ—alone—without the added filter of man's own interpretations and manipulations of the Holy Scripture.

I read Matthew 15 over and over again. I finally understood that if the Catholic Church was, indeed, one hundred percent spiritually correct in everything that it said and did, then certainly trusting the Catholic Church would in no way be harmful to my Salvation. But what if the Catholic Church was wrong, as I suspected that it was?

Many followers of Catholicism have been misled to believe that the way to God is through the Catholic Church. However, nothing could be further from the truth of God's Word.

> *"Jesus saith unto him, I am the way,*
> *the truth, and the life: no man cometh*
> *unto the Father, but by me."*
> *- John 14:6*

The Catholic Church also claims that it is the earthly representative of Christ, and that we should obey the church in order to follow Christ. In fact, the church of Rome claims that

Peter is the rock on which Jesus Christ founded the Catholic Church. Retroactively, the Catholic Church named Peter the first Pope. I say *retroactively* because the title of Pope didn't actually even exist until the Third Century. No papal doctrine is found in the Holy Scripture at all. Jesus Christ is the only foundation, the only way to God the Father, and thus is the only One we should follow.

The Catholic Church will point to Matthew 16 to show that Jesus founded his church on the rock, Peter:

> *"He saith unto them, But whom say ye that I am? And Simon Peter answered and said, Thou art the Christ, the Son of the living God. And Jesus answered and said unto him, Blessed art thou, Simon Barjona: for flesh and blood hath not revealed it unto thee, but my Father which is in heaven. And I say also unto thee, That thou art Peter, and upon this rock I will build my church; and the gates of hell shall not prevail against it."*
> *- Matthew 16:15-18*

At first glance, it may appear that Jesus was referring

to Peter as *the rock,* but we have to keep in mind that the New Testament was written in Greek. This is where the original wording reveals the true meaning of what Jesus had said. The Greek word for Peter is *petros,* which means *a small stone.* On the other hand, the Greek word that Jesus used for rock is *petra,* which means *a massive rock* or *bedrock.* Peter was correct when he stated that Jesus was the Christ. Jesus Himself is the foundation on which Christianity would be built.

> *"For other foundation can no man lay*
> *than that is laid, which is Jesus*
> *Christ."*
> **- 1 Corinthians 3:11**

If I accepted that the Roman Catholic Church *could* be wrong, at least wrong *sometimes,* then as a follower, how could I possibly know which issues the Catholic Church was correct about and which it was not? I had already learned that having the trees on the altar was in at least some way contrary to the Scripture. Dr. Lindstrom's CD had set me on a path to find out for myself that my salvation was permanent and not something I could lose because of my sin. It was also very clear that Christ Himself has told us that tradition is subject to the Word of God, not equal to it. Yet the Catholic Church insists that tradition and Scriptures are equal. Finally, I learned for myself that Peter was not the first Pope and was not the foundation of Christianity as the Catholic Church has long claimed.

Knowing that the Catholic Church was wrong about these things, what if the the Catholic Church was also wrong about others? Where should I place my trust, in the Catholic Church or in Jesus Christ Himself?

The church of Rome is led by humans who have flaws and can make mistakes. There are quite a number of historical errors within the Catholic Church, as most people may already know. But one thing I also knew for absolute certain is that Jesus Christ cannot make a mistake when it comes to God, while an organized religion on earth run by men easily could. I knew then, without a doubt, that when it came to my eternal life I simply could not take the chance on dividing my trust. I had to turn to the Holy Scripture for guidance and I had to trust fully, completely and totally in Jesus Christ *alone*.

That total and complete trust in Christ alone is the foundation of faith.

Once my eyes were opened I knew that I could not trust in the teachings of men *and* trust solely in Christ. As I've pointed out, there are times when there is disagreement between the two. Trusting in men as well as trusting in Christ meant that I did not place my trust *fully and completely* in Christ. It took me a long time to come to this simple and very logical understanding of the meaning of faith. Faith is putting all of your trust, one hundred percent of it, in Christ Jesus for your eternal salvation. Splitting your trust between God and man is faith that is not complete, it is divided.

Finally then I trusted in Christ *alone* and no longer placed any of my trust in the teachings of men. Finally I told Jesus Christ that I was willing to put aside the traditions of the Catholic Church and subject myself solely to the Word of God. Finally I told Jesus Christ that I trusted completely and only in Him for my eternal life.

It was only then that I was truly saved.

> *"Verily, verily, I say unto you, He that*
> *heareth my word, and believeth on*
> *him that sent me, hath everlasting life,*
> *and shall not come into*
> *condemnation; but is passed from*
> *death unto life."*
> *- John 5:24*

Jesus begins this statement with the words "verily, verily" which indicates to us that the words to follow are very, very important. Jesus tells us clearly in John 5:24 that anyone who hears His Word and *believeth* (trusts) in God (Himself) *hath* (has) everlasting life. Notice that Christ doesn't say "<u>will</u>

have eternal life" but rather "hath" eternal life. That's right, when we trust in Christ for our salvation, we receive God's Gift of eternal life right then and there. Not only that, but Jesus also assures us that once we receive eternal life we shall not come into condemnation, and at *that very moment* we are passed from death unto life.

Such a powerful, powerful assurance that Christ has given us. Once we place our trust in Him, we have eternal life. Something that lasts for eternity is something that will never end, that can never be taken away, a promise that can never be broken. How blessed we are to have that amazing life-changing assurance!

That night, for the very first time in my life, I truly received the gift of eternal salvation. Not in the future, not sometime after death, but right then and right there. I received it then as Jesus Christ promises us in John 5:24, and I still have it now, because it is eternal and it is something that will never, ever be taken away from me. Jesus says:

> *"This is the will of Him who sent Me:*
> *that I should lose none of those He has*
> *given Me but should raise them up on*
> *the last day."*
> *- John 6:39*

My life changed completely in that very moment! That night, I was born again. And just as God's Word promised, the Holy Spirit, the Comforter, came to be with me that night and I felt His presence near me:

> *"But the Comforter, which is the Holy Ghost, whom the Father will send in my name, he shall teach you all things, and bring all things to your remembrance, whatsoever I have said unto you."*
> *- John 14:26*

Because the Holy Spirit was with me and because I then began to finally truly understand the Word of God, the very next time I read the Holy Scriptures at home, alone in my room, I wept. I wept and wept, because everything had changed for me. I was finally saved and I finally understood everything that God my Father in Heaven wanted me to understand about my Salvation.

My life was changed for eternity.

* * * * *

Despite being raised a Catholic, despite being baptized

as an infant and confirmed in the Catholic Church, despite having been tasked with educating both youth and adult, that very night and for the first time in my life, I finally trusted that Jesus Christ paid my sin debt in full on the cross and that it was God's will that His son's sacrifice was enough to save me for all eternity. I trusted that Christ's sacrifice alone, through God's Grace, is the only way to eternal salvation and that there is nothing more that I could possibly do to add to it.

I finally trusted that nothing else, not my own efforts, not the sacraments of the Catholic Church, not the priest on the altar or in the confessional, nothing here on this earth could contribute anything more to my salvation. It is Christ's sacrifice and His sacrifice *alone* that saves us. I finally came to the realization that if I believed that my actions were necessary to save me then I believed that Christ's sacrifice *was not sufficient* for salvation. How could that be? Well, thanks to the Holy Scripture, we now know that it simply *cannot* be. My actions are in no way more powerful for salvation than God's Grace and Christ's sacrifice.

Finally I was truly saved, once and forever. And how do I know that my Salvation is forever? Because Christ Himself said so:

> *"Verily, verily, I say unto you, he that*
> *heareth my word and believeth on*

him that sent me, hath everlasting life,

and shall not come into

condemnation; but is passed from

death unto life."

- *John 5:24*

When Jesus is quoted as saying *verily* it is to indicate that what follows is very important. The original word is equivalent to the word *truly* in modern English. In this case, Jesus places great emphasis on his statement by using the word *verily* twice. He says that what follows is *truly, truly* real. Jesus also says *hath* (has) eternal life. Jesus doesn't say that everlasting life is something that those who trust in Him will have some time in the future. No, Jesus says that those who trust in Him *hath* everlasting life, right there and then, at that very moment. Can the Holy Scripture be any more clear? Jesus Himself stated the truth of eternal life in this very, very important passage. When we are Saved we receive the gift of eternal salvation, right then and there, once and for all, once and forever.

Not only does Jesus say that when we trust in Him we have eternal life, but that we shall not come into condemnation. At that very moment, according to the words of Jesus Himself, we are passed from death (which is being apart from God for eternity) unto life (being with God for eternity).

> "Then said he, Lo, I come to do thy
> will, O God. He taketh away the first,
> that he may establish the second. By
> the which will we are sanctified
> through the offering of the body of
> Jesus Christ once for all."
> - **Hebrews 10:9-10**

As we read in Hebrews 10, not only has Jesus come to do God's Will by sacrificing Himself on the cross for our salvation, but the offering of Christ's Body was made *once and for all*. That means He died once and only once, and through that single sacrifice all of our sins have been forgiven. Past, present, and future.

The Catholic Church refers to its daily mass as the "Sacrifice of the Mass":

> "The memorial of the Lord's Passion
> and Resurrection. The Holy Sacrifice,
> because it makes present the one
> sacrifice of Christ the Savior and
> includes the Church's offering. The
> terms holy sacrifice of the Mass,

sacrifice of praise, spiritual sacrifice,

pure and holy sacrifice are also used."

- Catechism of the Catholic Church[1]

But the Holy Scripture says that there was only <u>one</u> sacrifice:

"For by one offering he hath perfected

for ever them that are sanctified."

- Hebrews 10:14

How do we know that all of our sins are forgiven, even those we have yet to commit? Because all of our sins, every single one of them, have come and will come after Christ's one sacrifice. When He died on the cross, not a single one of us were alive. If it is God's Will that His Son should die for *all* of our sins, then it is for both the sins we have committed in the past as well as for the sins we have yet to commit. Truly this goes against the teaching of the Catholic Church, which contends that those who are members of the Roman church must confess their sins to a priest who gives them absolution for their sins, they must participate in their penance, and then they must receive the Body of Christ through communion to reach a state of grace and to have salvation. Once those Catholics fall into sin again, their teaching tells them that they must repeat the cycle in order to be saved. Yet this is not at all God's Will, nor is it what the Holy Scripture tells us about salvation. Jesus was sacrificed one time, once and for all. To believe that all of our sins are not forgiven means that we are attempting to sacrifice Jesus Christ over and over again.

> *"For it is impossible for those who*
> *were once enlightened, and have*
> *tasted of the heavenly gift, and were*
> *made partakers of the Holy Ghost,*
> *And have tasted the good word of*
> *God, and the powers of the world to*
> *come, If they shall fall away, to renew*
> *them again unto repentance; seeing*
> *they crucify to themselves the Son of*
> *God afresh, and put him to an open*
> *shame."*
>
> **- Hebrews 6:4-6**

Again, can Holy Scripture be any more clear? In Hebrews 6 we can read for ourselves that the Catholic teaching of a cycle of sin, repentance, absolution and salvation is *impossible*. Such a cycle simply cannot exist: the Scripture says that it is *impossible* to renew sinners again because to do so would mean that we would be personally attempting to crucify the Son of God for ourselves alone. Such a thing would be putting Christ's single sacrifice to an open shame.

With our new understanding of God's simple plan for salvation, and with our clearer understanding of the Holy Scripture, how can we continue to believe any earth-bound religion that teaches us that we must seek forgiveness for our new sins, over and over again? Jesus died for our sins, all of our sins, once and forever. Salvation is called "eternal life" because it lasts for eternity. If we were to receive salvation and then lose it again to sin, it would not be eternal. Therefore, to believe such a thing is to deny God's Will and to put Christ's single sacrifice to an open shame.

* * * * *

Even though I felt tremendous joy at my new found salvation, I was worried about the reaction my mother would have to the news that I could no longer remain a practicing Catholic. After all, though I'd been a Catholic for over forty years, she'd been a devout Catholic for more than sixty. She had raised her two sons to be devout Catholics, and was disappointed to see one of her sons fall away from the church. I would have to tell her that I too, like my younger brother Chris, was rejecting the religion that she had instilled in me since birth.

Still, I was almost busting with the good news of my salvation. So, knowing I couldn't wait, that weekend I decided to sit down and and break the news of my decision to leave the Catholic Church to my mother. I mustered up all of the courage I had and told her that I had something very important I needed to discuss. The only thing I could say to her was:

"I don't think I can be Catholic any longer".

CHAPTER SIX
Salvation and My Family

Upon my revelation, my mother asked how I came to make such an important decision. I told her that since my eyes had been opened to the truth, I could no longer simply accept everything the Catholic Church was telling me. I told my mother that I had begun to read the Scriptures more deeply and with greater understanding than ever before, completely unfiltered by the influences of any organized religion. I said that suddenly my heart was finally filled with the love of God and my mind was now open to the truth of God's plan for my eternal salvation. I told her that I had come to learn that some of the Catholic doctrines, traditions and practices were contrary to the Holy Scripture.

Then there was silence.

I was prepared for the worst, but her reaction took me completely by surprise. My mother told me that she had also been reading the Bible and re-assessing her spiritual life. She herself had started to doubt the teachings of the Catholic Church and some of the practices and behaviors she undertook as a Catholic. Her eyes were also now opened to the truth, and together we knew it was time to part ways with Catholicism.

My mother and I talked at length about the organized religion we were about to cast aside. There were important teachings of the Catholic Church that we found contrary to the Bible. On top of the teachings that differed from the Holy Scripture, one other thing bothered me, and that was how practically every single Catholic Church I'd ever attended had a huge crucifix erected behind and above the altar. My own parish was no different, in our church the image of the dead Christ hanging on that piece of wood dominated the altar. After I started to read the Scriptures for myself and learn the truth of God's Word—unfiltered by some organized religion's doctrines, teachings, traditions, and mistakes—I felt that the crucifix, the dead Christ, was not the sort of symbolism that my church would choose to present.

Christ Jesus died on the cross and through His sacrifice our sin debt was paid in full, that much is true.

However, the story doesn't end there. Jesus also rose from the dead, and to my mind, using the symbol of the dead Christ could de-emphasize His rising. The crucifix is a symbol that I knew in my heart I could no longer face. My Savior is *risen*, He isn't dead.

My decision has meant many changes in my life. The most important change is, of course, that I am now saved. I sometimes think about my more than forty years as a Catholic and I realize just how close I came to missing out on eternal salvation because I was being misled.

While my mother and I easily transitioned from our lives as Catholics, embracing our new-found Bible-based Christianity, the change appeared to be a bit more difficult for my wife and one of my teen daughters.

My youngest daughter easily accepted the fact that we would no longer be attending weekly mass, but she expressed concerns about how she was going to find the answers to her questions of the spirit. I explained to her that the Bible held all of the answers she would ever need, and that I would help her to find them. I assured her that between myself and my brother, we would be able to help her find her way.

My oldest daughter literally cried when I told her that as her father I could no longer allow her to participate in the Catholic Church. It was especially tough on her because she was in our parish confirmation class and her confirmation was just a few weeks away. My heart broke to see her suffer over my decision, but as a father and the spiritual leader of my household it was the tough decision that I had to make.

We talked and talked about this important change and how it affected my oldest daughter, and when we talked it all through, it turns out that she was not traumatized by being taken away from her church, but rather that some of her best friends were part of her confirmation class. In the end, she admitted that she was only distressed over the social loss, not the spiritual. Once she understood why she was so upset, she realized that she really didn't need to fret over it so terribly. Shortly thereafter she was Saved herself, and she has never looked back to the Catholic Church ever again.

Quite frankly, my wife and I clashed over my decision that our family would stop participating in Catholicism. My wife, who was also born and raised Catholic, demanded that I continue to allow my oldest daughter to attend her religious education classes and to complete her confirmation. She told me in no uncertain terms that if I refused to attend mass and refused to take my family to catechism class, she herself would do it and they would leave me alone at home every Sunday morning.

When she saw that I was going to be unmoved in my resolution not to allow my family to continue to be a part of Catholicism, she went from demanding to pleading.

"Can't you just allow her to have her confirmation?" my wife asked. "In a few weeks that will be over, and then we can leave the church. What's that going to hurt?"

I realized how important it was that my daughter not be confirmed a Catholic, and that my wife fully understand the importance and implications of my decision. My answer to my wife overcame her religious objections and touched on her sensibilities as a mother. I said to her:

"If you saw our daughter drinking something every week, something that she really likes to drink, and you suddenly found out that it had poison in it, would you stop her from drinking it immediately, or would you continue to allow her to drink it for just a little bit longer because it probably isn't going to hurt her much more?"

Far worse than poisoning her body, following the teachings of the Catholic Church was poisoning her spirit and preventing her from receiving the gift of eternal salvation. My wife then understood my position, she accepted it and eventually embraced it, and from that time forward we never again attended a Catholic mass.

CHAPTER SEVEN
My Life and God's Gift

You may be wondering how my life has changed since we left the Catholic Church. I say now with great joy that our Father in Heaven has blessed us more than I could have ever imagined. Myself, my mother, my wife, and both of our daughters all have received God's Gift of eternal life. All of us have even been truly fortunate enough to have the opportunity to share the message of salvation with others, and some of those people have undoubtedly been led to Christ.

Professionally, I had a high level position with a very respected financial institution, a company that I had been employed with for more than ten years. Because I was the department head of the company's technology operations, I was earning a very handsome six-figure salary. However, without realizing it, I had placed far too much emphasis on money and wealth and possessions. I owned a fancy custom-built home with a custom-designed ten-seat big screen movie theater. I bought a new car whenever I felt like it. I gave my wife and children expensive toys and gadgets. I indulged practically every material whim that my family and I had. My home was mortgaged for much more than it was worth, and I was heavily in debt with car loans, personal loans, and credit cards.

Despite having a great job and a high salary and all the material things I could have wanted, I was extremely unhappy, even though at that time I didn't even realize exactly how unhappy I was. My life was so centered around money that the first thing I thought about when I woke up each morning and the last thing I thought about every night before I went to sleep was our bills and debts and money. Every single day, despite earning a very, very good salary, I worried about how I was going to be able to pay to maintain our lifestyle.

During this time in my life, I was just beginning to experience the true spiritual joy that comes with being saved. Because I now belonged to the Body of Christ, God was speaking directly to me about my lifestyle, but I wasn't getting the message. My vision was obscured by my desire for the fancy material trappings of life and the quest for more and more money.

Finally, God made it clear to me how my emphasis on wealth was detrimental to my relationship with Him. He did this in my hour of desperation, as I searched for some way out of the financial corner I had painted myself into. My Heavenly Father revealed to me one very poignant verse from the Holy Scriptures that made His message to me as clear as it could possibly be:

> *"No servant can serve two masters: for*
> *either he will hate the one, and love*
> *the other; or else he will hold to the*
> *one, and despise the other. Ye cannot*
> *serve God and mammon."*
> *- Luke 16:13*

Mammon is a New Testament word which refers to material wealth which has an evil influence. And this one very simple passage from Luke truly hit me hard. So hard that I actually sat there for several moments in stunned silence. The message that God was sending me had finally gotten through: I was putting money ahead of Him. I was trying to serve two masters, God and wealth.

Immediately after I had read Luke 16:13 and finally realized that I strayed far from God's planned path for me, things started to change at work. I had spent my first ten years at my company, ten very happy and productive years, reporting directly to a senior vice president who I admired and respected greatly. We were almost always on the same page, and I supported him with all of my efforts. For those first ten years I was very proud of our company and proud to be in a respected leadership role within the organization.

About that time a new vice president was hired, and the reporting lines were changed. I was now reporting directly to the new vice president. It became evident from very near the start that I would be unable to professionally coexist with my new boss. It was clear from our dealings that my new supervisor lacked the same brand of personal and professional integrity that I shared with my former boss.

I had always been known as a very strong-willed leader. I possessed unwavering business and professional principles that I was unwilling to compromise. One day, my new supervisor confronted me behind closed doors and demanded that I put aside my own experience, opinions, expertise, and professional ethics. He made it clear that there was no room in the "new" version of our department for my unbending principles.

The reality of having to report to a vice president whose agendas and style weren't aligned with my own took a very heavy toll on me. Throughout my professional career I had always been virtually stress-free, but at that point, barely a year into my new supervisor's tenure, my stress levels had increased to the point that one night I actually ended up in the hospital. I was suffering from a severe outbreak of the shingles, which doctors told me was brought on by my work-related stress. The dangerous infection extended down from the top of my head and into my right eye. There was concern that I might end up with permanent vision loss.

Things then were about as bad as they had ever been, about as tough as I had ever experienced. But I never, ever gave up on God. He was the one I could turn to for a solution. I prayed and prayed for God's help. I asked him to heal my ailment, to eliminate the stress that caused it, and to restore peace to my life.

Fortunately, my prayers were answered in a major, life-changing (but totally unexpected) way. Within a few days of my return to work after having missed weeks because of my shingles outbreak, I was met in my office by my new boss and the director of our Human Resources department. They told me that the company was eliminating my position, and others, in a cost saving move. I no longer had a job.

Surprisingly, upon hearing the news that I would no longer be employed, I actually experienced a feeling of relief. I instantly felt a true sense of peace. In fact, the HR director, a woman who had been with the company only a short time longer than I had, was more shaken by my release than I was and she said so.

Because of my more than eleven exemplary years with the organization, I was offered a very, very generous severance package, which I accepted.

Just like that, my prayers were answered, but in a way that I hadn't anticipated. In a matter of minutes, my Father in Heaven changed the entire landscape of my life, as well as the lives of my family. God did for me something that I wouldn't have ever done for myself: he eliminated the source of all my stress and brought a new peace to my life by removing my stressful job.

God removed the source of my stress and anxiety, but He also made me deal with my rampant materialism. I don't think I would have ever left that job on my own. I'm certain that if it were not for God's intervention on my behalf, I would have continued to toil in stress, hoping and praying that things would get better.

For some, losing a high-paying job would likely be considered a curse, but for me it was a blessing. Just a few months after my position was eliminated, my brother Chris died of a massive heart attack at age forty-three. He had his own business, and because I was no longer working every day, I was able to spend a lot of time with him during those last few months. That time spent with him was an amazing blessing that I never would have otherwise had. It was truly a reward given to both of us by our Heavenly Father.

During my brother's life he had led so many to Christ, and I have to believe that his work here on earth was complete. I'm certain that he will spend eternity in the glory of God's Heavenly Kingdom.

I've chosen to share these details of my life because I feel it is important for others to understand how God works in the lives of those who belong to Him. He always knows what is best for us, regardless of what we believe is best. He always knows what we need, even when we don't. While we may be easily confused, if we trust in Christ and become a part of His Body, then we truly belong to God the Father and He will always be there for us, forever.

Dr. Hank Lindstrom has also passed away since I first made my personal salvation story public back in 2007. I was fortunate enough to share it with him before he died, and in turn he shared my story with listeners to his radio program and followers of Bibleline Ministries. I'll always remember his reaction to reading about my journey of faith:

"Truly this is one of the most inspiring salvation stories I've ever heard. Everyone should take the time to read this," said Dr. Lindstrom.

Now that my family and I belong to Christ's One True Church, which makes us a part of His Body, we spend more time together and much more time with God on an individual basis. Our relationships with our Heavenly Father has never been stronger or more personal. We've learned so much more about what it means to be Christians, and we've even learned how we should pray.

> *"And when thou prayest, thou shalt not be as the hypocrites are: for they love to pray standing in the synagogues and in the corners of the streets, that they may be seen of men. Verily I say unto you, They have their reward. But thou, when thou prayest, enter into thy closet, and when thou hast shut thy door, pray to thy Father which is in secret; and thy Father which seeth in secret shall reward thee openly.*
>
> *But when ye pray, use not vain repetitions, as the heathen do: for they think that they shall be heard for their much speaking. Be not ye therefore*

like unto them: for your Father

knoweth what things ye have need of,

before ye ask him."

- Matthew 6:5-8

Though I had stood on the altar in a Catholic Church every week, I never felt as close to my Lord as I do now. That's because now He holds me in the palm of His hand. Before, we may have spent an hour or so in church each week. Now I consider myself as being in church every single day, and I couldn't be more content. All of the financial stresses that I had piled upon myself have been lifted off of my shoulders by my Father in Heaven.

We now live a more contented life. Gone is the fancy over-mortgaged home with the movie theater. It was a house that always felt cold and uninviting. Instead, we now live in a warm, comfortable house that feels truly like a home. We no longer struggle with making massive payments to prop up a debt that was amassed to support an unnecessarily extravagant lifestyle. Our Father has blessed us with being debt-free, and we are never lacking. He always provides for us.

* * * * *

The spiritual joy I now feel, having learned the truth

about God's Gift of eternal salvation, is seemingly boundless. It is He who compelled me to share my story. I now have a closer and more personal relationship with my Lord than I ever had when I was a practicing Catholic.

And there's one very important thing that I want you to know, especially if you consider yourself a Catholic: my story is in no way "Catholic-bashing". I know that many of you won't believe me, but I tell you that it is absolutely true. This is a completely candid and personal account of how I decided to leave behind the teachings of the Catholic Church and to embrace a direct, unfiltered relationship with my Father in Heaven. I'm not Catholic-bashing for one very, very important reason: I know that almost every single practicing Catholic is sincere and truly believes that they are saved. How do I know this? Because I was one of them for almost forty-five years.

I have shared my story and these references to the Holy Scriptures out of love for those who have not been exposed to the truth of God's Word. I have shared my story because I am compelled to let others know that it is possible to have a direct, unfiltered relationship with God and that Eternal Life is available to anyone who seeks it out through the Holy Scriptures.

I praise the wonderful name of our Father in Heaven, and I thank Him for the incredible sacrifice His Son made on the cross for me, because through His death and resurrection my sin debt has been paid for in full, once and forever. I, and my family, have been born again in Christ. Because of His love for us, my family and I have all received God's true Gift of everlasting life. It is something that we have *right now*, as Jesus tells us:

> *"Verily, verily, I say unto you, He that*
> *heareth my word, and believeth on*
> *him that sent me, hath everlasting life,*
> *and shall not come into*
> *condemnation; but is passed from*
> *death unto life."*
> **- John 5:24**

I strongly urge you to pick up the Bible and read it for yourself. Research the passages I have cited for you, and take nothing I have said here for granted. Through the Holy Scriptures you truly can reach a real understanding of God's plan for your salvation. I know this because I have lived it. It was through this personal journey in faith that I have gone from *Catholic to Christian*.

* * * * *

The story is told of a man who was very eager to

attend a local revival meeting. Despite being so eager, he unfortunately arrived very late. Upon his arrival he found the workmen tearing down the large tent in which the meetings had been held. Frantic at missing the evangelist, the man decided to ask one of the workers what he could do to be saved. The workman, who was a Christian, replied:

"You can't do anything, it's too late."

Horrified, the man said "What do you mean? How can it be too late?"

"The work has already been done," the worker told the man. "There is nothing you need to do except trust in it."

CHAPTER EIGHT
Questions to Consider

After I had become Saved I finally understood that I was previously misled by an organized religion that wasn't completely true to the Holy Scriptures. Because of this realization, I was compelled to continue to do more research. I found myself looking into questions that I needed to answer not only for myself, but for others as well. What follows here are some questions that practicing Catholics should consider and pray over for guidance.

Where can we turn to find the truth about life's most critical issues of faith? There is only one source that will never mislead us, never deceive us or try to control us. It is Christ and His Word.

"Jesus saith unto him, I am the way,

the truth, and the life: no man cometh

unto the Father, but by me."

- John 14:6

And Jesus also said:

"If ye continue in my word, then are

ye my disciples indeed; And ye shall

know the truth, and the truth shall

make you free."

- John 8:31-32

I hope that you are ready to at least consider that the Catholic Church may not offer the best path to Salvation. I hope that my story might have inspired you to desire a more direct relationship with God. If so, then I ask you to please consider the following questions:

Question 1:

Why does the Roman Catholic Church
assign the title of "Father" to its
priests, and the title of "Holy Father"
to it's supreme leader, the Pope?

The Catholic Church uses the designation of "Father" and "Holy Father" despite the fact that the Holy Scriptures admonishes the faithful followers of Christ to avoid referring to mortal men as their "Father" when it comes to spiritual matters:

> *"And call no man your father upon*
> *the earth: for one is your Father,*
> *which is in heaven. Neither be ye*
> *called masters: for one is your Master,*
> *even Christ. But he that is greatest*
> *among you shall be your servant. And*
> *whosoever shall exalt himself shall be*
> *abased; and he that shall humble*
> *himself shall be exalted."*
>
> *- Matthew 23:9-12*

Here it is clear that we should avoid bestowing the lofty title of *spiritual Father* on anyone except for our Father in Heaven. No priest, no pope, no human being should be given the title of *Father* when it comes to our faith. Spiritually we have only one Father, our Father in Heaven.

Some will falsely argue that the Holy Scriptures, if taken literally, would admonish the faithful against even referring to their earthly father by that name. That argument carries no weight, because it is clear that the Holy Scripture here refers to the title of *Father* as it relates to our faith and our spirituality, not as it relates to our relationship with our paternal parent.

Question 2:

Why does the Roman Catholic Church require that its priests and other celebrants dress themselves in fancy vestments?

The Holy Scriptures tells us about the vanity of placing oneself above others and describes how these celebrants act and dress. This is much the same way that modern Catholic priests also act and array themselves in elaborate vestments:

"But all their works they do for to be seen of men: they make broad their phylacteries, and enlarge the borders of their garments, And love the uppermost rooms at feasts, and the chief seats in the synagogues, And greetings in the markets, and to be called of men, Rabbi, Rabbi. But be not ye called Rabbi: for one is your Master, even Christ; and all ye are brethren."

- Matthew 23:5-8

Question 3:

Why does the Roman Catholic Church
instruct its followers to continue to
make offerings for their sins through
penance, again and again?

The Holy Scripture makes it clear that God has made a covenant with us that because of Christ's single sacrifice there will no longer be any offerings required for the remission of our sins:

> "And every priest standeth daily
> ministering and offering oftentimes
> the same sacrifices, which can never
> take away sins: But this man, after he
> had offered one sacrifice for sins for
> ever, sat down on the right hand of
> God; From henceforth expecting till
> his enemies be made his footstool. For
> by one offering he hath perfected for
> ever them that are sanctified. Whereof
> the Holy Ghost also is a witness to us:
> for after that he had said before,

*This is the covenant that I will make
with them after those days, saith the
Lord, I will put my laws into their
hearts, and in their minds will I write
them; And their sins and iniquities
will I remember no more.*

*Now where remission of these is, there
is no more offering for sin."*
- Hebrews 10:11-18

To continue to believe that we must keep making offerings over and over again for the remission of our sins, we are denying the truth of God's own Words in Hebrews 10. God says that because of the one sacrifice of Jesus Christ, the sanctified are perfected *forever*. Because of this, our Heavenly Father says that He will *remember our sins and iniquities no more*. If that is true, and we know that it is because God does not lie, then how does the Catholic Church profit by requiring ongoing sacrifices from its faithful for the remission of sins?

By insisting that the followers of Catholicism must continue to make offerings for their sins, over and over again, the Roman church is creating an unnecessary dependency on the organization. Catholics who believe in this false doctrine are trapped into returning to the Catholic Church again and again, held hostage to an endless cycle of sin, confession, penance, and absolution dispensed by a priest.

> *"1497 Individual and integral*
> *confession of grave sins followed by*
> *absolution remains the only ordinary*
> *means of reconciliation with God and*
> *with the Church."*
> **- Catechism of the Catholic Church**[1]

Clearly the Roman church is attempting to circumvent the Holy Scriptures and create a false doctrine that requires absolution dispensed under the rules of the Catholic Church as the only means of reconciliation with God.

> *"Be it known unto you therefore, men*
> *and brethren, that through this man is*
> *preached unto you the forgiveness of*
> *sins: And by him all that believe are*
> *justified from all things"*
> **- Acts 13:38-39**

Nowhere in the Holy Scripture does it say that a priest is required to dispense forgiveness to us for our sins.

Question 4:

Why does the Roman Church insist
that Mary, the mother of the physical
body of Jesus Christ, is an active
mediatrix between man and God?

Catholics are taught that they can pray to Mary for her intercessions with God the Father, and that she is a *mediatrix* between God and man:

> *"(969) ...Therefore the Blessed Virgin*
> *is invoked in the Church under the*
> *titles of Advocate, Helper,*
> *Benefactress, and Mediatrix."*
> **- Catechism of the Catholic Church**[1]

Yet the Holy Scripture is, again, completely clear on the issue of exactly who acts as the mediator between God and man, and that mediator is only Christ Jesus:

> *"For there is one God, and one*
> *mediator between God and men, the*
> *man Christ Jesus; Who gave himself a*

ransom for all, to be testified in due

time."

- 1 Timothy 2:5-6

Clearly there is no other mediator named or necessary. We need not pray to any person, living or dead. All of our prayers should be directed to our Father in Heaven, through the Holy name of Jesus Christ. He will hear our prayers if we trust in Christ, and therefore there is no other person who is needed to intercede with God on our behalf.

What sense does it make to pray to Mary, the mother of Jesus, who is not herself an equal with Christ Jesus or God the Father, when we can pray directly to God the Father through Jesus Christ?

Question 5:

Why does the Roman Catholic Church
actively promote a doctrine that
supports the idea of a place of
cleansing called Purgatory even
though the Holy Scripture doesn't
mention such a place?

Purgatory is a Catholic doctrine that is unsupported by the Holy Scriptures. Purgatory is supposedly a place in the afterlife where some will spend time purging themselves of past sins so that they will be fit to enter Heaven. This doctrine assumes that we can somehow die in a state in which we are not good enough to enter Heaven yet not bad enough to go to Hell.

"The Church gives the name
Purgatory to this final purification of
the elect, which is entirely different
from the punishment of the damned.
The Church formulated her doctrine
of faith on Purgatory especially at the
Councils of Florence and Trent. The
tradition of the Church, by reference

> *to certain texts of Scripture, speaks of*
> *a cleansing fire:"*
> **- Catechism of the Catholic Church**[1]

In fact, there is no Scriptural support for any such place or state of being. For those who have received the Gift of Eternal Salvation, there is no additional cleansing required. To claim a requirement of cleansing for certain sins when it isn't at all necessary undermines the power of Christ's sacrifice.

> *"...the blood of Jesus Christ his Son*
> *cleanseth us from all sin."*
> **- 1 John 1:7**

1 John states it plainly and in a way that should not be misunderstood: the blood of Christ cleanses us from *all* sin. If we are truly cleansed by the blood of our Savior, Jesus Christ, how can it be that we will carry some sins into the afterlife that will require purging before we are fit to enter the Kingdom of Heaven? Only an earth-bound religion like Catholicism would espouse a doctrine that dictates that the blood of Christ is insufficient and that additional cleansing is necessary to enter the Kingdom of God. Again, through its erroneous doctrines and traditions, the Roman Catholic Church is making God's Word of *none effect* for its followers.

Question 6:

Why does the Catholic Church insist
on filling its halls of worship with idols
despite the fact that the Holy Scripture
forbids such practices?

As you may recall, during the story of my spiritual journey I wrote about walking the grounds of my church with my pastor and passing near a prominent statue of Mary, the mother of Jesus. Inside of our parish we had numerous statues on display, including likenesses of Joseph, Mary, several saints, and an interpretation of Jesus Himself.

Those who are familiar with Catholic churches know that most display statues and other images, including Christ nailed to a cross (the *crucifix*). Some Catholic Churches even have statues or portraits of living human beings on display, such as the Pope.

"Thou shalt not make thee any graven
image, or any likeness of any thing
that is in heaven above, or that is in
the earth beneath, or that is in the
waters beneath the earth: Thou shalt
not bow down thyself unto them, nor

serve them:"

- Exodus 20:4-5

Many Catholics will argue that the statues on display in their churches and their homes are not violating God's commandment against idolatry in Exodus because in Exodus God states that we must not honor or worship such images. However, the Catechism of the Catholic Church explains the purpose of these statues and images:

> *"1192 Sacred images in our churches and homes are intended to awaken and nourish our faith in the mystery of Christ. Through the icon of Christ and his works of salvation, it is he whom we adore. Through sacred images of the holy Mother of God, of the angels and of the saints, we venerate the persons represented."*
>
> *- Catechism of the Catholic Church[1]*

The Catechism states quite plainly that these statues and images are "sacred" and that Catholics "venerate the persons represented" by those images. The word *sacred* means *deserving of veneration*, and the word *venerate* means *to regard with respect; to honor; to worship; to revere.*

In order to provide more legitimacy to the widespread use of such images in Catholic Churches, ***The Traditional Catechetical Formula[1]*** as stated in the Catechism of the Catholic Church omits the portion of the Commandments of God that forbids the making of graven images.

In light of God's commandment in Exodus, do you believe that the Catholic Church is correct when it says that statues of Mary and angels and saints should be venerated?

What real spiritual purpose do such graven images serve when we know that it is only God that we must worship? Does having these images on display in your church or your home in any way enhance your relationship with Jesus Christ or God the Father?

Because of the existence of these statues and icons, many Protestants accuse practicing Catholics of idolatry. Since such opinion is so widespread, shouldn't the church which claims to be the one founded by Jesus Himself distance itself from the perception of idolatry?

"Abstain from all appearance of evil."
- 1 Thessalonians 5:22

Though God says that we should not make graven images and bow down to them, it is very common practice for

Catholics to bow or kneel in front of statues, particularly in front of statues of Mary the mother of Jesus. There are even many, many photos published of various Popes, the appointed leaders of all of Catholicism, bowing and kneeling down before statues of Mary. Clearly this practice and tradition is yet another act that is incompatible with the Holy Scriptures.

Question 7:

How did Sunday, the first day of the week according to traditional Christian calendars, become the official day of worship for the Catholic Church rather than the Sabbath day which is Saturday, the seventh day of the week?

In the New Testament, the seventh day of the week is referred to as the Sabbath. The Sabbath is actually mentioned nearly sixty times. The first day of the week is also mentioned a number of times in the New Testament, but it is called simply "the first day of the week" and it is always described as a distinctly different day than the Sabbath.

Jesus Christ made it clear that it is He who is the Lord of the Sabbath:

> *"And he said unto them, That the Son of man is Lord also of the sabbath."*
> *- Luke 6:5*

However, despite Jesus having established his exclusive ownership of the Sabbath day, Pope Sylvester officially named

Sunday "the Lord's Day" in the year 325 AD. Subsequently, the Catholic Church through the Bishop Eusebius, transferred "all things whatsoever that it was the duty to do on the Sabbath" to Sunday.

Effectively, the Catholic Church had decided to move the Sabbath from Saturday (the seventh day) to Sunday (the first day). This despite Jesus Christ Himself having staked His claim to ownership of that day.

The Fourth Commandment states:

> *"Remember the sabbath day, to keep it*
> *holy. Six days shalt thou labour, and*
> *do all thy work: But the seventh day is*
> *the sabbath of the LORD thy God"*
> *- Exodus 20:8-10*

Since the Fourth Commandment is quite clear about the Sabbath being the seventh day (Saturday), the decision of these Catholic officials to change the Sabbath from Saturday to Sunday demonstrates that the human leaders of the Catholic Church have *falsely* anointed themselves with what they incorrectly believe is the power to change the Commandments of God.

Question 8:

If the Roman Catholic Church is,
indeed, the one true church that was
established by Jesus Christ Himself,
how could it condemn Galileo's
discovery that the Earth moved about
the Sun rather than the Sun about the
Earth?

The trial of Galileo is one of the most embarrassing and infamous moments in the history of the Catholic Church. Galileo agreed with the assertion of Copernicus that the Earth was NOT the center of the solar system, and he went to Rome to try and convince the Catholic Church not to ban the work of Copernicus. Galileo was tried for his heretical beliefs, and he was held on house arrest for the final nine years of his life. The Church did not lift its ban on the idea that the Sun and not the Earth was the center of the solar system until the year 1758.

If the Catholic Church was truly Christ's real church and the Pope His true representative on earth, wouldn't God, the Creator of the Universe, enlighten the leaders of His church to the workings of the solar system so its leadership would not erroneously condemn those who spoke the truth?

Question 9:

*Why does the Catholic Church assert
that those who do not know Christ
can still achieve eternal salvation?*

There is one fundamental truth that should elicit agreement from even the most ardent Catholics: there is no salvation without the knowledge of Christ, because it is through our trust in His sacrifice that we are freed from all sin. Yet the Catholic Church says that those who are ignorant of the Gospel of Christ can still achieve eternal life:

> *"Those who, through no fault of their
> own, do not know the Gospel of Christ
> or his Church, but who nevertheless
> seek God with a sincere heart, and,
> moved by grace, try in their actions to
> do his will as they know it through the
> dictates of their conscience - those too
> may achieve eternal salvation."*
> **- Catechism of the Catholic Church**[1]

Again, this is yet another teaching of the Catholic Church that is contrary to the Holy Scriptures.

> *"Jesus saith unto him, I am the way,*
> *the truth, and the life: no man cometh*
> *unto the Father, but by me."*
>
> **- John 14:6**

Jesus leaves no room for any other interpretation or confusion. He states it as clearly as it can be said: no one can come to the Father except through Jesus Christ Himself. Jesus is the narrow gate, the only path to the Father:

> *"Enter ye in at the strait gate: for wide*
> *is the gate, and broad is the way, that*
> *leadeth to destruction, and many*
> *there be which go in thereat: Because*
> *strait is the gate, and narrow is the*
> *way, which leadeth unto life, and few*
> *there be that find it."*
>
> **- Matthew 7:13-14**

There are not multiple paths to Heaven. Any religion that teaches such a thing is teaching a lie. Jesus is the only path; all other paths aside from Jesus Christ are paths to destruction.

Question 10:

Why does the Roman Catholic Church
make a distinction between the
severity of sins?

The Catechism of the Catholic Church teaches that there is a distinction in the severity of sins. These are classified as less serious (*venial sins*) and more serious (*mortal sins*).

> *"1855 Mortal sin destroys charity in*
> *the heart of man by a grave violation*
> *of God's law; it turns man away from*
> *God, who is his ultimate end and his*
> *beatitude, by preferring an inferior*
> *good to him. Venial sin allows charity*
> *to subsist, even though it offends and*
> *wounds it."*
> **- Catechism of the Catholic Church**[1]

The Catholic Church claims that sins are evaluated according to their gravity and again, this distinction is a part of the tradition of the church. Not only that, but the Catechism also claims that this distinction is corroborated by human experience.

> *"1854 Sins are rightly evaluated*
> *according to their gravity. The*
> *distinction between mortal and venial*
> *sin, already evident in Scripture,*
> *became part of the tradition of the*
> *Church. It is corroborated by human*
> *experience."*
>
> **- Catechism of the Catholic Church[1]**

Yet this view of sin being distinguished by severity is contrary to the Holy Scriptures. Sin is sin, and all sin of any severity can separate us from God unless we trust in Christ.

> *"For whosoever shall keep the whole*
> *law, and yet offend in one point, he is*
> *guilty of all."*
>
> **- James 2:10**

That is why God the Father sent his only Son, Christ Jesus, to die for *all* sin, once and forever. No distinction between severity of sins is made:

> *"For God so loved the world, that he*

gave his only begotten Son, that

whosoever believeth in him should not

perish, but have everlasting life. For

God sent not his Son into the world to

condemn the world; but that the

world through him might be saved. He

that believeth on him is not

condemned"

- John 3:16-18

In addition, those who are made a part of Christ's Body by trusting in Him for their eternal salvation cannot suffer any condemnation, regardless of their sins, and regardless of some arbitrary human designation as to which sins are more severe than others:

"There is therefore now no

condemnation to them which are in

Christ Jesus"

- Romans 8:1

The idea that sins are distinguished by their severity is a clear example of human thinking and reasoning. It is the basis of the human system of justice, not God's plan for eternal salvation.

I certainly hope that you find these ten questions to be thought-provoking and worthy of further research, study and prayer. Remember that if you are prepared to follow Him, God will lead you where you need to go.

> *"Thus saith the LORD, thy Redeemer,*
> *the Holy One of Israel; I am the LORD*
> *thy God which teacheth thee to profit,*
> *which leadeth thee by the way that*
> *thou shouldest go. O that thou hadst*
> *hearkened to my commandments!*
> *then had thy peace been as a river,*
> *and thy righteousness as the waves of*
> *the sea"*
>
> *- Isaiah 48:17-18*

Father in Heaven, I ask that you please bless the readers of this text with the enlightenment to understand the real truth of your Word and the simplicity of your plan for salvation. Lead these readers away from all false doctrine and lead them along the way that they should go.

All praise, honor, and glory to God, my Father in Heaven. These things I pray in the wonderful name of Jesus. In Yeshua's holy name I pray.

Amen.

A Personal Appeal

To My Dear Readers:

I'm an independent author, which means that I choose to write and publish my writing without the benefit of agents or contracts or any sort of guarantee of compensation. Times are not easy for independent authors, but those of us who enjoy writing for ourselves and for readers like you value that independence.

I wanted to take a moment to ask you for your help. One of the most important things an independent author can have are <u>reviews</u>. Reviews help readers decide whether or not they should make an investment in reading a book like this one. All reviews are very important to authors, the most glowing praise and the most scathing comments are equally welcomed.

I know that what I've written here isn't for everyone, and I truly respect all opinions on my work. If you believe in and support independent authors like myself, then I ask you to *please* take the time to rate my book where you acquired it.

Most sellers such as Amazon make filing your review of this publication very easy. It usually takes less than one minute of your time. Whether you enjoyed this book from start to finish or whether you couldn't stand to read another word, won't you please take just a few moments and write a brief review? Your assistance in this matter is vital to the on-going success of independent authors.

Thank you,

S.C. Slawin

References

All Bible references are taken from the King James Version.

[1] **The Catechism of the Catholic Church**
http://www.vatican.va/archive/ENG0015/_INDEX.HTM
Retrieved January 2014

[2] **The Council of Trent**
Session XIII - The third under the Supreme Pontiff, Julius III,
celebrated on the eleventh day of October, 1551
http://www.ewtn.com/library/COUNCILS/TRENT13.HTM
Retrieved January 2014

[3] **Polls and Statistics**
THIRD GALLUP POLL (1992): BELIEF IN DOGMA ON
HOLY EUCHARIST
http://www.traditio.com/tradlib/polls.txt
Retrieved January 2014

My Personal Gift to You

If you enjoyed reading my journey of faith, then I would
be pleased to offer you a no obligation **FREE GIFT**.
To claim your free gift immediately, simply visit:

www.CatholicToChristian.com

Made in the USA
Middletown, DE
20 May 2023

31002805R00076